I0161336

Influence
&
Leadership

Mike Cornwell

Sanctuary Leadership Publishing
Mountain City, Tennessee

Copyright © 2021 Mike Cornwell
All rights reserved. No part of this book may be reproduced in any form without permission, in writing, from the author, except for the use of brief quotations in a book review.

For more information, Sanctuary Leadership Publishing can be reached at publishing@sanctuaryleadership.org

ISBN 978-1-7366826-0-9 (paperback)
ISBN 978-1-7366826-2-3 (hardcover)
ISBN 978-1-7366826-1-6 (ebook)

www.mikecornwell.com

Cover design: Mike Cornwell
Interior design and composition: Rick Soldin

Printed in the United States of America

Dedicated to my dearest Julia,
whose first "I Love You Daddy"
touched my soul,
and forever changed me.

Contents

Acknowledgment

As I write this section, smelling bacon from the kitchen, it's clear that I need to thank my wife most of all who, without her assistance on every real front, there would not be enough time to have written this book, let alone accomplish much of what is accomplished.

This book was made possible entirely through reflecting on the people who have impacted me over the years having, proven beyond a shadow of a doubt that leadership is a phenomenon that moves mountains.

I want to thank my dad, Bud Cornwell, for standing as a paragon of virtue and family values. The realization of the importance of character and its proof of influential abilities could not have been possible without your tireless patience.

I want to thank the many leaders (military and civilian) who have made an impact on me to the point where this book could be inspired and realized. While there have been many in my life, I want to specifically thank the following:

- Dave Warman
- Michael Niermeier
- Mark Shepard
- Tom Aiken
- Michael Cmeyla

- Chris Honaker
- Dan Pena
- John Maxwell
- Daron Long

Introduction

> *"For unto whomsoever much is given, of him shall be much required: and to whom men have committed much, of him they will ask the more."*
>
> —Luke 12:48

Hello, my name is Mike Cornwell, and it's my life's mission to super-charge and defend invaluable rural landscapes. I am achieving this by influencing the actions of myself and others.

Everything in this book is designed to help you answer the only three questions relevant to leadership:

1. Why is it possible that every person can be influenced?
2. How do I earn the ability to direct someone's actions?
3. How do I direct these actions for the right reasons?

In 2019, I decided to make a major change in my life. The clarity that can only be provided by a vision of purpose demanded that I write this book.

The various enterprises that I had built over the last five years have been put on an indefinite pause to write this book. This book takes what is often represented as a hazy subject and distills it down to the fewest points that anyone needs to know. The compelling causes to write this book are sufficiently important enough to no longer leave the future just to chance alone.

You see, in the preceding years, nearly every step that I have taken has been down questionable roads. In some cases, I did not want to take a path and did so anyway. In other cases, the "thing" that I was presented with was too interesting not to pass up, even if I *knew* that my life was destined for something else.

Subconsciously or consciously, I have always known that there was something else that I ought to be paying attention to and working for with extreme haste.

As they say, it would be the path least traveled and most needing of blazing.

Nobody *needs* another micro-brewery. Nobody *needs* more reasons to hop on their digital screen devices. Nobody *needs* to spend their life in a rat race created by other humans who are high in cleverness and low in morality.

What people *need* is a belief in a real future. People need to believe that their work matters.

The Now is Pressing

The most recent turn of events has created the pressing need to move with swift haste. Of all the rabbit holes I have found myself in, **this** one is perhaps the most disconcerting. I have gone from building vibrant edible ecosystems across the Southeast United States to helping a global terrorist organization in the middle of its bureaucratic collapse.

There are many unproductive and destructive organizations that litter the globe and are hungry to bring in someone, anyone, to help them with their problems. Yet their problems aren't from a lack of talent; it's from a lack of leadership. Their failure is of lack of vision, purpose, and connection to people.

The great organizations that occupy our planet are operated entirely on fearful auto-pilot. They are staffed from top to bottom by people who are led by fear and, in turn, spread these fears onto those beneath them, very similar to a man-made virus. Yet, worst of all, they have no positive vision for the future; in turn, enlisting your mind, body, and life to produce a darker future for all stakeholders, inside and out.

The associated problems that come from an absence of leadership are *here* on our doorstep *now*. Those with inquiring eyes need only look at the land around you to see this evidence.

Our Lands Are Missing Organic Intensity

With the proper training and awareness, if you look around, you will see land dominated by unproductive, poorly grazed pastures, scrub growth reclaiming land opportunities hard-earned by those in the past, and a near-impossible feat to transfer of land assets to the next generation of motivated land stewards.

As a result, the prosperity of the future worldwide is being paved over everywhere for cheap, mass-produced homes.

There are a multitude of reasons why these problems are on our doorstep. Some are conjured from the imagination of stagnant and purposeless minds, and others are the result of organizations too bloated and now primed for destruction. In a few cases, there are problems created by those with a thirst for destruction who simultaneously have the knack for getting cooperative people to follow them.

Until recently, my concern was not wanting to be known for "a thing" that I invented or designed. Whether it's my fruit experiments in Southern Louisiana, my deep dive into apple genetics (planting over 200 varieties), the ecosystems I have built and consulted on, or even my first attempts in business by writing a book geared to suburbanites on a dubious chicken raising system called chicken tractors.

Upon reflection, I realized that building a more stable future by working on trees and environments alone would not bring about a vision for a better future. Instead, I knew that I had to utilize the lessons gathered during and since my experience in the Marine Corps to grow people to influence not only their environments but others around them.

What matters is people and what they spend their time doing.

*Where are people who have the highest ethical character? Where are people who have their shit together enough to **help other people**? Where are the people who have a compass strong enough to lead people?*

From long consideration after the micro-success and closing of my Permaculture fruit tree nursery business, I have come to a much clearer understanding of why I could not affect the level of change in people's lives that I was trying to create.

I was going after the symptoms and not the root problems.

While selling near-extinct fruit trees to the public, the following questions would continually crop up:

"Why are people not planting trees in mass?"

"Why are people not taking responsibility and ownership of their lives at a much higher level?"

Cultivating people into their finest is far more important and valuable than growing food, fiber, and medicine systems around where you live (What is arguably the single most important activity humans could be engaged in at this moment in history.)

You might ask, why focus on people?

"Many hands, make light work," but the only way to make those hands constructive, instead of destructive, is to learn to lead.

Know that this book was written to speak to you.

It turns out that I know why you're reading this book. The desire to change our surroundings is in-bedded deep within us. We, us humans, are makers of the world, and we have not only the ability but the destiny to create a beautiful world to occupy.

I know the experiences in this book can help you.

This book's concepts are as plain as they can be. You should be able to take any part of this book, take what you read, apply it in the real world, and see the results for yourself. The world will shape around you differently as you use the contents of this book.

You must know that the information contained in this book does not come from abstract education lessons and did not come from the prevalent group think of today. Instead, these writings come directly from me to you.

I am an actual active practitioner of influence who just happened to gain consciousness of the craft that I employ.

It has brought me abundant opportunities, adventures, friends, riches, faith, hope, and even humility.

This book is a distillation of *what I know*, without necessarily the full story of how I acquired this knowledge. While those stories are of value, you must know that this book provides much of the source code of what it takes to shape the world around you.

These, often unconscious elements, spelled out here, have created an environment of safety for those who are around me. During the "pandemic" of 2020, it would be near impossible to have fear while around me. Because of my lack of fear and the overall drive towards the initiatives we have been focused on for years, there is simply no time to give credence to what is being said "out there." Aided by my wife, who is naturally happy-go-lucky, those who come around get pulled away from the world that is provided to them on an easy-to-digest emotional platter and are entered into a world of planning, production, and big thinking.

This is the world that I live in.

Sure, I could avoid taking responsibility and believe it is entirely by chance that somehow those around me aren't concerned about "what's going on out there." Or I can accept the truth that leadership has once again accomplished its purpose, its job to funnel the minds and activities of others towards better and bigger ends.

I believe that leadership is the answer
to *every* human problem.

This belief runs contrary to the three prevailing beliefs of how to solve human problems.

Science and technology: These are the pathway to better tools. What good are tools if they don't serve the purpose you are after?

Education: While it's important to improve our ability to learn, too much classroom time creates a belief that *knowing details about a problem is the same as knowing how to solve them or* **knowing whether there is actually a problem to be solved at all**. There is a philosophical argument that has not really been universally settled that asks, "can you determine what you should do, based on what facts you know." From what I've gathered about the arguments, you cannot *know* what you should do from the facts. Instead, what you actually do is determine what you should do based on what you already value. The facts are there just to support your reasoning. **Education is, at best, a comfort blanket.**

Business and "Capitalism": This pathway leads to a functional exchange of goods, which depending on the way the wind blows, results in *corrupt, hollow human behavior. If you look, you will discover a pyramid of deception and aggressive tactics used to manipulate people for personal gain.* The not-so-saintly "powers that be" *believe/d capitalism can and should be harnessed for good.* Building societies around this is a debated topic.

These three approaches have been cornerstones to the narrative of growth for the past 200 years. To that I have there is the saying:

"What got you here won't get you there."

If you think there are issues in the world, you're not alone. There are, but they cannot be solved by more of the same. We don't lack

the technology, we don't lack education, and we don't lack a desire for people to make money. We are lacking in leadership, influence, and action. The world is lacking the fullest *you.*

You May Be Wondering, "Why Me?"

Why should *you* be the one who dawns the mantle of leadership? Why should you take ownership of every interaction that you encounter with others?

Don't we have governments, non-profits, and large corporations that all have systems to "prevent people from falling through the cracks", "solve world hunger", or "cleaning up the environment"?

There is an endless stream of politicians and celebrity personalities who are trying to redirect the efforts of these large systems to do what they believe is good in this world. So perhaps it makes sense to turn over these efforts to them?

Why should you help the poor that you see if there are homeless shelters, they can go to or government programs and handouts? Shouldn't they all "just go get a job and stop being lazy bums!"

Have you ever considered that, maybe, it's the reliance upon these systems and abdication of responsibility that *are* the problem?

Have you considered that an individual's belief in large unaccountable entities arrests their God-given will to act? Have you considered that yielding over yourself to large unaccountable entities might be abdicating your connection with your fellow man? A keen eye will understand why it is a futile effort to leave large legacy organizations to the task of helping people. These activities are, in fact, not their purpose at all.

It is *the organization's purpose for existence* that sets all future actions and limits their change. The following list is the missions of these large organizations:

- Governments exist *to control* by gaining and using military, political, and economic force.,

- Corporations exist *to make a profit* through the accumulation of resources for as cheap as possible and then selling them for as high as they can.

- Non-Profits exist to make donors smile and feel good about themselves.

These organizations are drowning trying to achieve even these missions. Is there any real surprise by their inability to solve problems that, in many cases, are contrary to their own existence?

Instead of focusing on giant unaccountable bodies, let's focus on the real world:

Friends go home feeling alone and resort to drinking.

Family members go to bed wondering if anyone loves them.

Great ideas evaporate because their creators lose spark and give up, even when they are moments away from victory.

These situations exist because leadership is absent. If you fill the role of leader in your life, your mere existence will bring light and drive to others.

Contained in this book is both the understanding of why this is the case and what you need to do to unlock them.

Leadership Involves How You Interact with Others

The contents of this book is for you. This book is designed to give you the essentials to lead effectively, whether you are new to leadership or you have been leading for a lifetime. It does this by helping you understand how to connect with yourself and others for the purpose of earning the ability to influence them towards goals that you envision. In order to build these solid leadership foundations, the book is organized in the following sections:

1. Know the Foundations of Leadership
2. Influence Yourself
3. Earn Influence with Others
4. Spending Influence
5. Become an Effective Leader

This book contains only the essentials necessary to build influence and deploy it.

This book is *not* written with statistical information, facts, and scientific literature to "convince" you that what is in this book is real or that it works. After beginning the application of artifacts found in this book, you will discover for yourself these truths.

Dear reader, know that it is the current zeitgeist and groupthink to believe that only magical white-scientists can tell you about the world.

What do you see in the world that should be rearranged?

Should our countrysides flourish with productivity? Should nature be growing in the complexity of animal life and species rather than diminishing?

You may wonder what these questions have to do with consciously leading. If you ask questions about the improvement of the world and wonder how to improve things that are greater than yourself, it requires growing into a leader to solve them.

Everything truly worth doing requires more than you to accomplish; ergo, you need other people to help. **But what are you doing to get them to work for your cause?**

There are only a few ways that work to earn a person to your side and complaining that "somebody ought to do something" isn't one of them unless you want them to complain that "somebody ought to do something." The section "Earning Influence: Consistently and Strategically" explains how to get them to listen to you, and then "Spending Influence: Wisely, Honorably and Purposefully" explains what you ought to point them to do.

Let's Focus for a Moment

Instead of just integrating with the world of humans (such as reading this book) and reacting to everything you hear, just stop.

Stop.

Relax and allow yourself to be detached and watch what is going on. Instead of going along with the groupthink that focuses the attention of everyone on *distant issues*, focus on what is going on *right in front of you, right now*.

Think, feel, and examine what is happening right in front of you, with **real** people you can see and hear. Maybe even do it as though you are a third party who is completely invisible.

What are the people in front of you doing, and why do they behave this way? Why do you think they behave in these predictable ways instead of any other way that you might imagine?

Then, I would suggest you go further and ask the question…

What does it mean that they do *this* all the time?

This is the question that ought to bother you at night. A keen thinker may then apply that "if these people do this, then does this mean that the majority of people do similar things with similar results?"

The answer is an unbridled "**YES**."

If there are patterns that people do, then there are patterns to being able to interact with them that have relatively predictable results.

This is why you can learn to influence people. In the section "How People Work", you will learn why people are doing what they are doing. By learning these major points, you will be able to insulate yourself from unproductive thoughts about others and allow yourself to lean into the innate traits of people. This is part of gaining a consciousness of your efforts. The lessons will open up your ability to lead them.

Should You Lead?

You and those you come into contact with can obtain your strongest desires through leadership. Whether or not you can see through the fog created by endless distractions or whether you can compel others to act big and small is up to **you**. Regardless that which is bigger than you can only be achieved through leadership.

Before we really get into the discussion of leadership, just know that it is a naturally obtainable skill. For me, it started as a natural skill that I began to intentionally develop. At first, it started with getting small pleasures in life, but eventually, I realized that the unconscious application of influence and leadership returned **sporadic results, failures that spanned over years, and not meeting my fullest potential, let alone helping anyone to develop theirs.**

I'm not going to beat myself up about that which I didn't know about, and neither should you.

The skill that I have been employing for over three decades, which until recently was performed part-time and unconsciously, is called **leadership.**

You would think I would have picked that up while spending time in the Marine Corps from 2004 to 2010, but I had not understood leadership as a discipline at the time that I should spend much of my focus on. It turns out even in a leadership-oriented organization; the world will rarely and sporadically stop you and explain what is really going on.

Only after you know *that some people are operating entirely with the mindset to influence you, can you understand how the world really turns.*

Leadership is the only skill that has the potential for keeping human life moving in a better direction.

The absence of leadership is decay and collapse. The presence of leadership leads to prosperity.

It *really* is that simple.

If you have been raised to think that you can just become an employee at a company, do the work you're told, and create prosperity, you need to know that you are sadly mistaken. Life is far more complex and rich than an idea so simple. This idea benefits the leaders that are trying to simplify your existence for the benefit of where they are taking everyone.

Having "A Job" As Your Ultimate Goal in Life is Beneath Your God Directed Existence. Arise!

Employees have a glimpse in playing a part in prosperity because leaders charted the course of improving human life and made sure people had what they needed to carry on.

Behind every improvement, there is a leader. Behind every expansion, there is a leader. Behind every change that has ever happened, good or bad, there was a leader. The larger the effort, the more **leaders** it took.

It's not like leaders are performing magic; it just requires someone to have the end in mind and willing to spend their time influencing *others* to move in that direction.

When business leaders stop leading, employees run on autopilot, problems are no longer solved but tolerated, opportunities are no longer sought out, and **the entire business decays and collapses.**

That is just an example from business, but it applies to absolutely every human endeavor. Betterment is pointed to by a leader, who then rallies others to build the success that is possible. If the leader has not cultivated another person to lead after them, the previous successes fade.

A leader is a necessary catalyst for any bigger purpose to materialize.

Here is what I can tell you:

- Leadership is a skill
- Leadership can be learned and practiced by everyone, including you
- The world needs YOU to be a leader, NOW

Let's Focus on The Road Ahead

Whether or not you are a leader now or not is irrelevant to the text before you. This text serves as a strong foundation. Trust that this book is filled with intentional influence, even from the time you first encountered it until the time you put it down.

As a reminder, the book is formatted in the following compounding structure:

1. Know the Foundations of Leadership
2. Influence Yourself
3. Earn Influence with Others
4. Spending Influence
5. Become an Effective Leader

Without any further adieu

Know the Foundations of Leadership

Leadership is Influencing Action

"Leadership is influence, nothing more and nothing less."
—John Maxwell

Leadership is the ability to influence people to take action. The purpose of leadership is to compel action on a purpose that is larger than oneself. A person who has the ability to get others to act is called a leader. A follower is a person who is highly influenced by a leader. *Everyone* can become a leader of someone else.

The acquisition and deployment of influence are required to unlock the actions of others. This influence is gathered by earning it through actions performed for another person's benefit. Influence is then exhausted each time a person is asked to perform an action.

Leaders understand what people do and why they do it while simultaneously seeing these aspects in themselves. Conscious leaders intentionally use these human aspects to choose the best available methods for earning and expending influence.

In order to influence others, a leader must be able to effectively influence themselves. This is done through the process commonly called building character.

Two effective ways to earn influence are taking continual small actions over time and making selected intelligent actions with strategic importance. The results of these methods are limited only by what you can conceive and physically perform.

Lastly, influence is best utilized wisely, towards an honorable and purposeful end. This purposeful end is an intentional change in the configuration of the universe that provides a better, more desirable future for many. It can be either abstract, such as the adoption of particular morals and values, or concrete, such as the creation of a building. People are only attracted to a leader because of their desire of beneficial, honorable, and purposeful ends.

This is all there is to leadership.

While leading is a complex activity, at its core, leadership is neither complicated nor mystical. Leadership is simply the act of influencing others. Those that do it well *know* this and are intentionally seeking influence for their cause.

It can be difficult to pinpoint a leader. Leaders can speak loudly, and other times leaders speak softly. The leader of a group can be easy to spot and yet sometimes impossible to find. Some leaders do not know that they are the leader.

Yet what identifies the leader is the influence they earn and then exert on others. It is only influence that defines a leader.

CHAPTER 1

Influence

Influence is a relationship dynamic that provides the ability to compel a person to do an action, behavior, or hold an opinion.

This relationship dynamic is the currency of a leader. This relationship currency flows in and out of a leader's control to empower one person and then to empower another. Influence is collected over time and spent by directing a person into action.

Because influence is a relationship dynamic, it is obtained only through interactions with each and every person. It is possible to influence others indirectly from information shared by those who are influenced; it is not possible to take influence earned with one person and expend it with another. This is where the currency analogy ends.

Influence is *just* a relationship dynamic.

Know this. Influence is actually practiced by everyone. Whether it is getting someone to believe that it is OK for you to be late for dinner or whether they should charge a hillside in a military battle, both individuals are using influence.

Influence begins at the basics, like being willing to help a child tie their shoes or being willing to "go first" when things are not so certain. These small actions send clear signals to others, telling them, "this person cares about me." Once a person has the eyes and ears of another person, they have the *privilege* to use that influence to get them to do actions of their choosing.

The difference between great leaders and the average person expending influence is the great leaders *intentionally*, continually, and strategically work to earn influence while spending their influence wisely with purpose.

This is precisely why scandals involving leaders are truly bad.

Large scandals occur when a person who intentionally built influence over years decides to use their earned influence to do something less than honorable for perhaps no meaningful purpose. **The tragedy is the influence and earned trust have been squandered.**

Everything a leader does, they do because it either earns or spends influence. This is why a leader cannot be identified by the specific actions, they do; rather, it is the "*why*" they're doing it and the intended effects it will have on others. The same person can do two completely opposing actions and yet it can still make sense. A leader will only "lead from the front" if the person believes that taking action and being observed doing it, will **influence action**. A leader may stay in the rear because the leader believes they have enough influence to get the action purely by spending their influence.

The Role of Force and Fear

Force and fear are complicated tools grabbed far too often. The conscious leader takes great caution about utilizing these tools because of the effects on followers.

Fear is the feeling felt by a person when they believe "if I don't do this, then bad things will happen to me."

Force is the act of coercing someone to do a particular action. It does this by instilling an immediate sense of fear.

Force may get a follower at *that* moment to do an action, but it will not propel the person to push forward when they're no longer forced. The act of using force "spends influence", reducing the total influence the leader has over the other person. Eventually, this influence is drained to none, resulting in the person fighting back.

Force creates ill-feelings and hatred for the leader and, even worse, completely abdicates the followers from taking ownership over the actions they are performing. Therefore, using force requires leaders to use an unlimited amount of energy to continue to propel a person forward, effectively making $1 + 1 = 1.5$.

There could be nothing more toxic to a leader trying to earn influence and wisely spending it than using force.

> The tighter one grips, the more chaos spills out of
> the hands until there is nothing that's in control.

You may hear people argue that you *can* use fear to "motivate" people because "people are motivated by fear." Leaders must guard themselves carefully against these claims.

Fear, **a negative feeling,** is toxic to the follower. Those on the path to leadership will adopt a sacred duty to seek a sense of responsibility for followers. It is the leader's job to steer around obstacles and detriments, including the impacts of fear.

A consciously aware leader addresses fear directly because they know that empowering a follower to overcome fear makes them *effective*.

The Incontrovertible Evidence that Influence is a Truth of Goodness

Keen eyes will spot a peculiar truism in influence. Influence as a phenomenon of human existence remains eternally real and tangible.

Consider for a moment...

Why is it possible that people can be influenced *at all*?

Is it not odd that for some reason, certain persons can compel much from us, while others cannot?

How is it possible that you have inside of you, right now, triggers that can set you off on a new vast journey, just from a single encounter with the right person?

We all are able to be influenced because we are looking for others to validate what we believe and show us a way to obtain that which we want most.

Even if we are closed off too much of the world, we can still be opened up by the *right messages* at the *right time* by the *right people*. Because we have desires in life, *is why influence works at all.*

Therefore, leaders and budding leaders must know where they are trying to go so they will know how to influence themselves *first*. Then a leader will be able to communicate to others that they have a better chance of getting where they want to go, if they go through you.

Is Manipulation Influence?

Some mistake intentional influence for manipulation. Manipulation is the act of finding what a person desires, using it to make them believe they will get it so they will lend their strengths, and then never delivering on the promise. As a result, manipulation is harmful to people, and in the long run, harmful to the practitioner.

People believe manipulation works *because it does*. Manipulation works because it taps into the same areas where influence works. Manipulation rides on life's desire for survival by cooperation.

However, using manipulation results in temporary solutions to what are often long-term problems.

Manipulation never has the ability to obtain something greater than oneself. It can neither forge trust nor allow for continued returns. Manipulation is the basis for a shaky foundation built on deceit; a foundation built on sleight of hand does not have the fortitude to stand any resistance.

Similar to fear, manipulation will accomplish individual tactics at the expense of long-term strategies.

Leaders must remain vigilant against using manipulative tactics. This is accomplished by staying focused on the bigger picture, improving communication and character while staying square with one's message. Followers themselves should be able to track every task back to the bigger effort. If they cannot, they will not have the ability to autonomously act, instead waiting for every arm-twist or manipulation scheme to make them move.

CHAPTER 2

Action

Action is the tangible mechanism that creates influence and therefore makes leadership possible. People are only influenced by the physical actions that others do. It is through actions where influence is earned, and it is through actions where influence is spent.

Effective leaders use actions consciously to build influence with others. Small and continual actions reassure people of a leader's care for them, while strategically selected actions can build lifelong trust.

It's not just any action that earns influence. The actions that matter are ones where the results can be seen and felt by others. While there are many impacts actions can have, influence is built from the actions that others *desire, wish for, and need.*

Take the following everyday situations:

- Staying late to help someone else with their problem.
- Providing a listening ear during a tough time.
- Saying a bold statement in public.

These simple everyday examples have great impacts on the psychology of others. Through just these three actions, others will know that what's being done comes from a place that cares about **them.** For those willing to take these actions, they will not only earn a friend, but the privilege of authority to change their mind, redirect their actions, and even realign their direction in life.

It is the impact that actions have
that cause influence.

This is why we are looking for actions seen and/or felt. It is not the action *itself* that matters, but how the action is perceived by the recipient. While actions do not need to be personally witnessed, there are powerful effects with actually **seeing** someone perform an action. The sight of action compels a person to become influenced. In other words, the sight of action creates the possibility of others taking action.

Creating witnesses is the single greatest
influencing tactic that can ever be
performed by a leader.

Seeing is powerful because we trust our eyes more than any other aspect of our being. Instead of hearing stories, which often are doubted, seeing an action performed becomes an undeniable bedrock from which influence springs into existence.

There is a "Compounding Effect" to witnessing an action. If an action is performed by more than one at the same time, it has an even greater influence on those witnessing it. Instead of believing "only they can do it", witnessing others sends the signal, "maybe I should do this too."

People may doubt their ears, rarely do they
doubt their eyes, but never do they doubt
their eyes among **many.**

Influence Tip: Compel Others with Compounding Effect

If you need others to accomplish a task where nobody is compelled to do it, you can get them to join by using the compounding effect. The compounding effect can be created by first **starting** the task. Then ask for assistance from a person who is more easily influenced. You can now take a step back and ask for others to join in. Almost like magic, those who said "no" and were against helping will fall in line, and in many cases, with enthusiasm. The more that start, the more that will pour in.

While seeing a leader perform the action is the gold standard in influence, it is ***not*** a requirement for creating influence. Let's demonstrate this by letting your imagination work for you.

If you close your eyes and work your imagination, imagine how the following actions would impact you personally:

- You are told by the bank that someone paid your debts.
- You receive the job you wanted because someone put in a good word for you.
- Following your recent big promotion, you receive a letter from someone very important congratulating you.

How would you physically feel in these situations? If you noticed, in all of these situations, the person performing the action was never observed. Yet, in these real situations, the recipient remembers that "someone" fondly for their ***entire life***.

The actions that influence cause emotional reactions. The ones that earn the most influence are the ones that deeply send the message **"you matter"** and **"it's going to be OK."**

> Those who desire to become leaders need only change their actions. Leaders who desire to grow and become greater leaders need only change their actions. To accomplish the greatest goals we desire in life; we need only to change our actions.

Is Planning Action?

Planning is a thinking activity. **While there are other reasons to conduct planning**, people often plan because they are trying to *raise their personal confidence* and *reduce uncertainty felt now and in the future*. This is why people on the verge of popping can exclaim, "*we have to have a plan!*"

Where people run into issues is they try to replace necessary action with planning.

Planning can make you feel like you are doing something. Planning can make you feel like you are interacting with the future. And planning can make you feel like you are in control.

However, the person who plans is *planning*. They are not interacting with the future; they are interacting with models that *represent* the future. And unless the planning results in creating enough influence within oneself to take actions, the planner is neither in control of the universe nor themselves.

> Those who perpetually plan without taking
> further actions neither raise their confidence
> nor reduce uncertainty.

Planning is an important activity in getting familiar with what comes next; however, it is no substitute for what comes next.

Are Words Actions?

The phrase "actions speak louder than words" speaks to our intuition that words are rarely enough to cause the change we seek. It is true that words are the most used method for trying to win others to our side. Because words are easy to use, their use is often ineffective. However, words are still actions.

> Underneath every word spoken, there is an
> underlying action taking place.

This act of speaking is a "conveyance" or the passing along of something, which happens to be the emotional state of the person speaking.

Similar to a subtext in a piece of writing, what is being conveyed is rarely what is being explicitly stated. Careful listening and observation can give clues to **understand** what a person is saying. However, the listeners' natural reaction shows what is actually conveyed.

The emotional state of the speaker merges with the emotional state of the listener, causing distinct and often predictable reactions.

The action that influences is the reaction caused by the speaker.

The following list distills nearly every communication between humans into its actual action:

1. Increase or decrease confidence in oneself or another.
2. Increase or decrease fear, uncertainty, and doubt in oneself or another.
3. Increase or decrease the belief of interest in a person.
4. Increase or decrease the amount of joy/excitement in oneself or another.

Leaders and those new to leadership need to take the above list seriously. Before speaking, consider which of these are you going to convey. Before responding to someone who just spoke, which of these are you *actually* about to convey to them?

Are you in the process of denying someone their beliefs and opinions, causing them the need to rise up to maintain their confidence? Or are you making a bold, prideful statement in front of someone thinking that it will raise their confidence in you?

The following is a **sincere word of caution:**

Speakers are rarely aware of what actions they are producing. Without knowing it, when people speak, they often convey low confidence, a high belief in uncertainty, and a disinterest in the person listening. Contrast this with what they are saying, such as "they have confidence", "everything is OK", and the person in front of them "means everything to them."

> These common speaker mishaps can *spend influence rather than earn influence because it demands the listener believe something they do not already.*

Instead, speaking ought to raise confidence, reduce uncertainties, and make the listener leave feeling as though there is interest in them.

Detailed strategies and tactics on speaking and listening are provided in the section on Earning Influence with Others.

Influence Tip: Speaking Directly to People

If you listen to what the other person needs (confidence, reduction in uncertainty, or interest), you can craft a message for them specifically. When people speak, they are often expending influence, which is your opportunity to pick it up. You can do that by identifying what emotional state they are in, addressing it directly, and then telling them that you have high confidence in them. If you raise up others, you will earn influence.

In Summary, Leadership is...

Leadership is the practice of conducting continual and strategic actions that earn influence with others, which is then used to compel persons into wisely chosen actions that have an honorable purposeful end.

In order to become a leader, you must adopt an attitude of growth, be of good character, have a genuine concern for the wellbeing of others, and continually seek progress towards a purposeful end.

To effectively lead, you need to understand the complexities of how people operate, become aware of these peculiarities in yourself, and assist in searching for and maximizing the expression of each person's innate qualities.

Influence Yourself

Fortifying Your Personal Character

*"Waste no more time arguing about what
a good man should be. Be one."*

—Marcus Aurelius, Meditations

CHAPTER 3

Who Are You?

No really, who are you? What drives what you do? Have you considered that people not only act differently, but think differently, believe differently, see different facts, and even *see* different things in the world? In a very hazy and topsy-turvy world, knowing who you are, is more important than you might first think.

If you do not know who you are *now*, you will not know what skills you should be using and improving, you will not know which skills you should avoid, and you will not know how you come across to others.

As this text progresses, consider who you are, it will give you your next stepping-off point for fortifying your character.

Leadership Hint: Admitting Fault Influences Growth

Acknowledging that your personal character is in a state of improvement can be difficult. But remember, you're signaling to the world that growing is better than being stagnant, and even if you make mistakes, it's better to try and fail than it is to not try at all.

A Person's Character is Their Most Influential Quality

It is a person's character that has the most influential power. A person's character shows up day after day and shows who the person consistently is. Your personal character will determine the actions that you take, how you will speak to others, and how others interpret what you're doing.

If you have great and superior character, people will know. If you have poor and inferior character, people can determine this as well.

This isn't necessarily a conscious process. As you communicate with people, they are not spending their time understanding why they like somebody; they just do. If asked, they'll rationalize why they are attracted to a person, but at the core, it's their character.

A person's character matters more than their titles

A person who is of poor character placed into a position of "leadership" will inevitably fall from grace. *While position definitely gives one an added advantage at influencing,* a person's character will ultimately be why they continue to be influenced. Poor character results in poor actions, which results in people turning away.

A Man of Poor Character

There was a man who had poor character. When he first started a new job as a team lead, he commanded people's attention, and they listened to what he had to say. They believed in his confidence about what he thought the team should be doing to earn their employment, even though it was counter-intuitive. While he possessed some leadership traits, his poor character showed up more often than his leadership abilities.

Every day he would leave work exhausted and frustrated.

Each morning he arrived at work with bright ideas that he believed would turn everything around. Because these ideas "were so good", he commanded other people's attention to listen to them. Over time he commanded more and more time. Yet each time, he found resistance to these ideas and quickly become frustrated over their lack of acceptance. Daily he concluded that other people are too emotional or fundamentally flawed to understand even simple ideas.

But the problem was not other people's lack of intelligence or their emotions; it was his personal character.

He was unaware of how his poor character daily translates into actions that negatively impact the lives of everyone. Because he believed that it is some else's fault, he removes his ability to make *real* changes that can improve his life and others.

His character told others that people are not the greatest asset; instead, they are obstacles to be overcome. This is why he regularly found himself in debates and publicly reprimanding. *His poor character led him to believe that emotions are problematic and an obstacle rather than a useful means for influencing.*

A person of poor character cannot see how **their own negative emotions** cause negativity in others that only are eventually reflected back.

Overall, this person's character is preoccupied with *itself*, leaving no room for the attention of others, and finds itself unable to figure out how to influence those around him.

Before we continue down the path of influencing others, we have to talk about how our personal character shapes us.

Every single day, your character influences you.

While your personal character speaks volumes to others, it speaks volumes to yourself. Remember, leadership is about influence. In order to influence others, you must absolutely influence yourself first. Your character is what propels *you* to take action. This includes actions that others will not take if it weren't for you taking them first.

If a general could not get themselves to storm a hill, why would they be able to get others to do so?

If dishes aren't getting cleaned currently, and you won't clean the dishes, why do you think that anyone else will all of a sudden decide to do them?

Your character is composed of your past actions, and these past actions set the level of difficulty that you play life on. People can see your character becomes it comes out in the way that you live your life. It also comes out in what you accept out of others. As a result, the work you spend fortifying your own character sets your ability to perform great actions or small actions.

This is why it's imperative to improve your personal character.

Your Emotional State Matters to Others

Do you take responsibility for the emotional state of others?

As in, when someone is having a bad day, and they do something bad as a result, do you take responsibility for it? Or do you point the finger and say, "oh, it's that person's fault. Everyone is responsible for themselves." Know that those who take responsibility for the emotions of others know they can cultivate their own emotional state to steer a group towards success.

This shouldn't sound farfetched.

All people are intertwined. Everyone has the ability to modify the group's emotional and cultural dynamics. Some view this as a problem where other people weigh them down. Others, leaders, view this as the ability to test your ability to lift others up. Emotional state is shared, and you have the ability to modify the emotional state of those around you.

> ### Influence Tip: Detecting Influence Levels
>
> You can quickly gauge your general influence level if you see people's problems as annoyances or opportunities. Practitioners of influence use the struggle of others as an opportunity to earn more influence. As written, this may seem manipulative or "capitalistic", but it's really accepting that during hard times, people appreciate the support and assistance from others. It just so happens when you help them, they'll like you more.

You Don't Need Perfect Character

You need the character that says, "character matters and improvement is valuable". Even if you do not have perfect character (no-one does), paying attention to character begins to show to *yourself* and others that who people really are is what matters. By vocalizing that personal growth is important and healthy, it gives you the opportunity to try harder and even fail.

Even the struggle to improve character, a shared struggle, earns you influence.

Even if you are struggling with character development in your life and happen to communicate it with others, it tells them that something bigger than your current self is valuable, and you're humble enough to see you're not there yet. This makes you approachable, and belief, growth, and transcending petty problems is possible.

Sharing struggles gives people hope.

Your struggles in life will influence people who know you personally

Your struggles are not always important for influencing everyone, but people who truly want you to succeed will appreciate that, every day, you'll work through your own struggles. It gives them the strength to work through their own. Just by you working on your tough issues, it will give breath for others to work through their own.

You see, humans are all interlinked in their efforts, and oftentimes and we can get too analytical about what's going on around us. We can read too many books, we can see too many movies, and we can get turned around about how things work.

Yet, people respond to what they see and what they absolutely know.

They do not need any explanation of the activities that are innately human. And let's remember that influence is a human activity. By influencing yourself, you'll influence others to be able to influence themselves as well. If you're working on your own personal growth, others will be able to pick up on it. If you talk candidly about your struggles, it will create an environment where other people will talk candidly about their own struggles.

Influence Tip: Struggle Shares

This tactic, known as a **"Struggle Share"**, is a good way that you can learn about other people. Sometimes asking is good, but other times leading by example is even better. Sharing our experiences in life will engage people's minds to think about their experiences and report them back to you. A small recommendation is to avoid providing "assistance" or "recommendations" on how to improve themselves unless they ask for it or really give you an indication that they want you to comment. Internal struggles are often personal battles that people feel they need to win themselves. Just you providing an ear alone is assistance.

CHAPTER 4

Your Character is What You Stand For

Are you a person of virtue? Or are you a person of vice?

Are you a person who is obsessed with personal pleasure?

What are you not willing to do to get what you want?

Are you so weak in your own confidence that you believe that only by helping others does it make you a good person?

If you do not earn influence with yourself continually, strategically, and daily, you'll find that getting yourself to action **will be met with resistance.**

This is why people feel lazy.

To improve one's character, every single day, you have to continually influence yourself to get to higher levels of performance, whether that is through technical improvements or preparing and challenging yourself mentally or physically.

Getting an understanding of who you are, in all your faults and flourishes, is important towards direct yourself to a higher level.

You see, we take ownership of our destiny whether we think we do or not. Every day, we make decisions, small and large, that put us on the path to become who we will become. Every day we're changing, but what is changing is up to us.

> Who are you? What do you value? Who do you
> want to become? Answer these questions first to
> yourself and then to others, and it will set you on
> a path of influence.

CHAPTER 5

What are Values

In simple terms, values are intangibles that people like and deem valuable. These intangibles often interweave together, called "**a value system**". Value systems are what people use to make daily decisions without having to question or second guess themselves.

Because people make decisions based on value systems, every activity performed by a person is an expression of what they value.

Do you like frosted flakes, cheerios, or none of the above?

If you do like them, why?

Because you ate them as a kid and have fond memories or because you think they taste good?

Did you like them at one point in time but no longer?

This example should show you that even the act of eating a box of cereal shows something about what you value or what you valued at some time. You may value eating sugary foods, but you might not later. You may value living "in the now" versus eating for the future. You may like frosted flakes because your father liked them, and you value your father and family.

What we all do, is an expression of what we value.

Do you know what you value?

Actions Speak Louder than Words

When you're trying to understand the values of others or even your own, be careful when listening to what people profess about what they value. As with any self-reported information, often, but not always, what is said is different than their behaviors. Take note that speech itself is a behavior but taking what people say is often foolish. Studying and analyzing what people actually do will make it clear what they value.

A Small Value Analysis Example

Imagine you have two men that work together in a larger team, Stan and John. John is appointed to be the supervisor and superior to John and the team. Stan is trying to understand what John values so that he can influence John (his supervisor). Stan notices that John **dresses much nicer than others, gets frustrated quickly when working with different types of people, and has odd quirks about his behavior.** It is not uncommon for John to bring up the topic of leadership and influence with Stan and the team.

"I pay attention to the needs of those under me. It is other people's work, not mine, so that is why you'll see me give credit for it." John says.

While John says this, Stan notices that John **does not see if his subordinates need equipping, tasks the team to make his responsibilities easier, and often berates individuals in the team publicly.**

Stan attempts to use *all* these bits of information to derive what John values and does not value. Here are Stan's conclusions about John.

1. John values the way he makes himself look.

2. John values acting as an individual.

3. John values his own ideas.

4. John values the perks of being put into a position of leadership.

5. John values verbal discipline.

Ultimately, Stan cannot find how John values other people and instead finds that John just values himself. Even though John verbalizes the value of leadership, his behavior shows habitually that he does not.

It is unknown what is really going on in John's head. It is possible that John believes he is a great leader who is very capable of influencing people. Stan could ask; however, the answer is always filtered through John's relationship with Stan and John's self-projected image to the world.

This is why taking what people say literally is a bad idea. If you are ever in doubt, remember, actions speak louder than words.

Since actions speak louder than words, if you want to communicate your values effectively, using actions is the best way to do it. Words can be used to call people's conscious attention to the actions you perform. *However, calling attention to yourself will backfire against you if people do not believe that is what actions you are performing.*

Influence Tip: Feedback Networks

If you are interested in as realistic and direct of feedback as possible, build a feedback network. First, build deep trust in a few people. Next, ask these people to discover what others think about you. It is really easy to fall into the trap of worrying "what other people think about you", but that isn't what should be conveyed here. Rather, you are making sure that you have a two-way understanding of how your actions match your words.

You Need to Know What You Value

If you don't know what you *already* value, you need to begin that discovery. Create as exhaustive of a list as you can of what you value. I would recommend trying to get to the highest-level abstract values rather than detailed ones. Example:

Instead of saying:

"I value my parents."

Write the following:

"I value family."

Try to be thorough. By doing this, you will begin to see what values are most important to you. Seeing these values will make you become consciously aware of how these values manifest in your daily life.

Can your values change?

Values can and do change.

Do they come from birth? Do they come from family? Do they come from friends?

The answer to all of these and more is "yes." Values can even come from books read, and experiences gained. If you have a hard time coming up with a list, consider the lists that will be presented next as a starting point.

You need to know what you value.

CHAPTER 6

The Marine Corps Leadership Traits

The following are *leadership* traits that are taught by the United States Marine Corps. When I was first introduced to these traits, I thought they were "good to know", but not something necessarily to take seriously.

I do not hold such a light opinion anymore.

The following list should be memorized and worked into practice constantly and daily. You may be asking, "why are they so important?"

These are the character traits of leaders.

When these traits are displayed, they earn influence with those around you. If for no other reason than to earn influence, these traits should be learned and applied daily.

Influence Tip: Utilize More than Teach

While talking about these values with others is important for spreading the knowledge about these values, it is far more important to utilize them. Displaying them by performing acts is a necessary requirement for others to adopt these values. People follow the leader's example, so if you want others to adopt good traits, you have to display them yourself.

1. Justice	8. Enthusiasm
2. Judgment	9. Bearing
3. Dependability	10. Unselfishness
4. Initiative	11. Courage
5. Decisiveness	12. Knowledge
6. Tact	13. Loyalty
7. Integrity	14. Endurance

Justice

Fairness and Accountability

Justice is the act of treating other people fairly. This includes praise, rewards, and holding others accountable.

Justice requires looking at each situation with people from a light of understanding and then taking the appropriate next action based on the facts learned.

If you act justly...

It will help you create harmony. This harmony helps your endeavors in at least two ways.

1. It helps foster a harmonious environment where people are willing to trust and act in their fullest capacity.

2. It reduces the amount of bickering and "talk back" when actions and decisions are made.

Judgment

Make a decision, known

Judgment is the act of making determinations. Oftentimes people will wait and require an unending amount of data in order to make determinations. This is called "analysis paralysis."

Judgments and decisions clear uncertainty and focus everyone in a particular direction instead of other directions.

If you make sound judgments...

People will respect you and listen to what you have to say. Get used to the fact that some people require considerably more information to make them feel comfortable; however, when you have proven that your sound decision-making works, even those who are the most risk-averse will come around to you.

Dependability

The Core of Trust

Being dependable means that others can trust that you will be there when needed. People must believe that you will stay true to your word, no matter what. The consequence of not being dependable is losing trust. If people lose trust in you, they begin to shut you out.

Life adapts to its surroundings; this includes people's character traits.

If you are not dependable, people will assume this and begin to work around the fact that you are not dependable. They will do this by no longer bringing things to you that matter. You may even end up in a bubble, protected from all issues because you cannot handle them.

By being dependable...

You will earn influence easier, and when you spend your influence, it will require less. Imagine not having to spend a considerable amount of time convincing people to do something. This comes about by earning their trust.

Initiative

The act of moving with purpose

Initiative is the character trait of seeing what's in front of you and making a move rather than sitting and waiting. Leaders who take initiative move faster and are able to get ahead of the changes in their environment.

Initiative gives a leader the ability to lead yesterday and today and push forward to tomorrow. Taking the initiative gives the leader the ability to interact with others on the ground and the timing of the leader's choosing.

Initiative is a requirement for getting relationships unstuck and out of unproductive and debilitating habits. By taking the initiative, a leader has the ability to spot the changes that are needed, and instead of waiting around, will seek to make the changes.

In order to earn respect among those whom you lead, you will need to take the initiative with them personally. Good and bad. One example is holding them accountable. It is very important to hold a person accountable and to do so as soon as it makes reasonable sense. Taking the initiative allows the leader to make the right impact when it's most relevant.

Influence Tip: Accountability Shows Care

Even if you cross people whom you care about by taking the initiative, it still shows that you care about them. This is one of the odd paradoxes that "nice" people miss. Giving a person a hard time "just because" is one thing (don't), but giving a person a hard time by holding them accountable for the things they have said they would do, is a necessary requirement for taking leadership. People need a person who is skillfully capable of handling lapses in judgment and action and are willing to help them get over the issue. Without accountability, the person's character withers. Just note, there is a happy middle ground between being loved and feared where being most effective lives. Being loved makes people not take you seriously, and being feared makes you impossible to follow.

The last statement to make about initiative is that people who take initiative know more than others. Instead of having a passive approach to learning, they move forward and find out for themselves what is really true. Those who waste time sitting on their hind end stating something can't be done could instead move forward to determine it themselves.

If you act with initiative...

Nobody will doubt that you are there, and you are a force for good. Even if you are clumsy at first, initiative earns you influence with others instantly. People usually don't just hop in and get going, but you can.

Decisiveness

Quick, Definitive Decision Making

Decisiveness is coming to decisions quickly and definitively. If you have made a decision, make others know about it.

Making decisions based on having 60% to 80% of the needed data seems to be the sweet spot. Decisiveness requires intuition in order to know when to stop analyzing and move onto action.

There is no shortage of people that won't make a decision, and even if they do, they keep it to themselves. It is the easy thing to do.

If you act decisively...

You can get on with getting to the "hard" parts of life and finding what you ought to be doing and the direction that you need to be going in. Acting decisively reduces uncertainty significantly, which, as we've learned, paralyzes people and saps their energies. I hate to say it, but for many people, they'd rather be working away on something that doesn't matter than waiting around for the perfect tasks to come their way.

Get people moving in the direction they ought to be going! Now!

Tact

Sensitivity for Others On Difficult Issues

Tact is the finesse of working with people on difficult issues. How you act or react when others are frustrated or sensitive determines your ability to influence them. Having tact means that you understand what concerns them, that you demonstrate that you are considerate of their feelings, the matters at hand, and your responses are in-line with being productive and moving forward.

People appreciate it when someone is willing to engage in a difficult conversation with them while respecting them at the same time. It's not easy, but well worth the investment.

When you show you have tact...

People will begin to treat you with respect and listen to you. People can tell when you are going to lengths to respect them. **This earns you influence.** Realize you can truly steer your destiny, and **even when you need to have a tough discussion with someone, you can still earn influence in the process!!**

Integrity

Strong Moral Principles

Being a person of integrity means that people **know** they can come to you. They **know** that you represent doing things the mature, responsible way and that you can handle it. Integrity means standing strong based on moral convictions, even when it's inconvenient for others. Poor integrity leads to being influenced to do things that one shouldn't.

You can dramatically earn influence with people by standing up for what's right and holding others accountable for what they say. Integrity is integral to a solid core.

When you have integrity...

People know they can count on you. Trust in you will increase, and your influence can be earned continually. Integrity reduces uncertainty because people know exactly where you stand and what you will and will not tolerate. As a result, other people will start taking on the same attitude of tolerating this, but not that.

Enthusiasm

A Contagious Thirst for Life

Enthusiasm is required for performing at one's highest abilities. And it's contagious as well.

Enthusiasm becomes truly necessary when we are starring at a task that we don't necessarily want to do. It is in those moments that enthusiasm is needed most. By having enthusiasm, others around you, who may be feeling unmotivated to perform a task, will begin to pop alive. The enthusiasm is for the sake of others.

There are many stories of veterans who were out on patrol, demoralized, and without any desire to be there who turned things around with enthusiasm. The leader identified a slump in his men and decided to start making jokes about what's going on. This built an internal excitement for what they're working on, and as their enthusiasm increased, their energy and will to survive also increased.

When you have enthusiasm...

You will earn influence with people who need it. Enthusiasm is contagious and is life-enhancing. Tasking people when you are enthusiastic also reduces the cost of spending influence. For some reason, when a person is really enthusiastic, it is hard to tell them no.

Bearing

How Do You Carry Yourself?

Your bearing is the way that you conduct and carry yourself. It is the way your inward qualities express themselves to others. "How you conduct yourself" will become what people know you for.

Do you get hot-headed when someone does not do exactly what you wanted them to?

Do you attempt to cheer others up when they're down, or do you pile on them?

People are watching, they're judging, and they desire more than anything that someone has the internal fortitude to be able to handle the problems of the day.

When you have strong bearing...

It reduces uncertainty. People know what they are going to get from you. They know that you are going to do your best to point them in the direction that you know and will only change when it makes the best sense. As long as you remain true and solid, you will continually earn influence.

Unselfishness

People follow those who do things for others.

The secret to leadership is doing actions for others. Make no mistake about it; influence is earned from actions in the service of others, which requires acting "unselfish."

People instinctively know that the common action among people is to look out for themselves, to do the selfish action. This is why doing unselfish actions are so powerful.

Unselfish actions stand out.

One simple example is opening a door for a person: instead of doing it just when it's convenient, doing it when it's inconvenient for you. If you see someone struggling, run out ahead of someone so you can get the door for them. This additional step makes quite the impression.

When it is 100% clear that you do not benefit from doing an action and that only others benefit, without any explanation, people recognize this internally.

If you haven't already, begin watching people's lives and what they expect out of the world around them. They receive less and less, and the world is becoming so much larger than everyone. In this kind of world, people rarely are truly complimented and are thus not deeply appreciated. This is fertile ground for behavior that puts others first, something that never happens for them.

If you act selfishly, you'll fit in. **But if you act unselfishly, you will pop out and shine.**

Those who are unselfish...

Can unlock people much easier. Earning influence is an absolute breeze and spending it requires so little. If there is any characteristic that will earn you the most with **other people** in life, it is being unselfish.

Courage

Earning influence when it matters most

You can tell when you are about to do something that requires a bit of courage by the amount of butterflies in your stomach and the nagging feeling in the back of your consciousness that makes you hesitate to go further.

Regardless of feelings, this is the time to act.

People respect courage. The courage to say what many are thinking and feeling but won't say. It's courageous when you are willing to step out in front, be the focal point of attention, and perform an action that bolsters and emboldens everyone.

Courage is a lifelong pursuit that requires consistent pushing of one-self beyond the boundaries.

For me, one such example was in Marine Corps boot camp when the squad leader and guide mafia decided that they wanted to start picking on someone. While our platoon was split off into groups inside our squad bay, the recruit "leadership" decided to start patrolling around, making sure everyone was "doing what they're supposed to." They saw my friend writing a letter in his notebook instead of working on memorizing some information.

Instead of using leadership and influence, they decided to use violence by kicking him in the chest. Rather than stay silent to the abuses of power, I stood up and confronted them in front of the entire platoon. I questioned their power and made it known that behavior was inappropriate. That one situation was the end of it, and eventually, the guide and squad leaders begged me not to tell on them since they knew that they would have to start boot camp over if the instructors had found out.

This story isn't to draw attention to myself but rather a daily real-life scenario that demands courage. Standing in true defense of persons and people is almost always courageous behavior.

Courageous actions don't always result in the possibility of violence, however. Most often, courage is needed to do small things, like asking questions. For some reason, looking "stupid" and feeling as though you are being judged by others is very heavily weighed when deciding to speak.

Those starting out in improving their courage should seek public speaking opportunities and change the way they respond to when your body starts getting fuzzy and full of butterflies. Start by doing an action that leans into those feelings rather than desiring escape.

If you act courageously...

You will earn influence with all those who see it or hear about it. Those who follow in your footsteps will be able to act with an even greater ability. Seeing is believing; seeing earns influence, and there is no doubt that courageous actions earn influence.

Knowledge

People who know are valuable, people who don't are obstacles.

Knowledge is the combination of validated information and personal experience. While there are many definitions to knowledge, this is a more stringent definition than a casual one. This know of knowledge is difficult to obtain because it requires taking added and extra steps of information gathering and personal validation.

Information is not knowledge.

Unlike the many forms of information, knowledge is extremely important. Leaders ought to seek it out constantly and never assume it can be just "given" to someone.

When people erroneously believe that knowledge can be passed like information, they believe they can delegate the gathering of knowledge to others. As a result, this person has no idea what's going on, and every time they speak, they lose influence with those who actually do have knowledge.

Knowledge, rather than information, is required for the following reasons:

1. Having knowledge is the best way to tackle solving an issue. Having enough information (60–80%) is required to do something intelligent rather than foolish.

2. You can be a person who can accurately identify what's going on. Important information will not leak nor change because you understand enough to keep everything in context.

3. You are able to keep the people around you accountable by understanding more than just enough. You need to be able to call bullshit.

Acquiring knowledge ought to be a lifelong pursuit. If you're not reading books, taking classes, and engaging with other people about what they know, and seeking out the truth yourself, you will have no ability to rise up.

You don't need to be the smartest or the most learned; you need to be smart enough on what's going on, so people are capable of following you.

Warning: Knowledge has a side effect...

There is a trap in believing, even with justifications, that you know a lot. When people learn a lot, people often feel the need to share this information with everyone. It is easy to see in the real world that some people love to tell others about what they know that they think others don't. Often unasked. But consider for a moment.

> If they are speaking, they are not listening. If they
> are not listening, they are not learning. If they
> aren't learning, they aren't gaining knowledge.
> Those who speak too quickly know too little.

By acting with knowledge...

You will gain a strong and true footing in the world. People will trust your judgment and decisive action. Knowledge is a trait that helps every other trait do its job better. Knowledgeable people earn influence just by existing and being a resource for others.

Loyalty

If you're loyal to them, they'll be loyal to you

Loyalty is the act of showing continuous support for a person, organization, or idea.

Loyalty is a critical component of influencing others because it is a necessary requirement for a culture of trust. At its bare minimum, loyalty gives a rock-hard foundation for people to build together, so even if things fail, you can still depend on each other.

Loyalty builds a culture of resiliency in the face of any situation. Loyalty, especially when it's inconvenient, is one of the acts that people remember most.

"When things were bad, he could have switched jobs. But instead, he was there for us when we needed him most."

Loyalty is like the dependable trait, except that it focuses on being dependable to *specific people*.

The easiest way to get others to be loyal is when you decide to be loyal first.

In order to build loyalty, you must start by letting people know that you value them and are willing to stick with them even if it gets tough.

When presented with an "opportunity" to shy away from your loyalties, such as bad-mouthing a person behind their back, you must resist and overtly state that you will not.

Loyalty doesn't magically happen. It's a conscious and continual effort to influence yourself, to remain loyal to those around you who matter. Just ask those who have been long married.

Those who are loyal...

Do not seem to lose influence as easily. Loyal people can make mistakes and be forgiven, again and again. When you are loyal, you earn influence from others consistently. They know you will show up when needed most.

Endurance

People follow those who never quit.

Endurance is the mental and physical stamina to keep pushing through even when it's tough.

Endurance is a requirement for getting anything difficult accomplished, whether that is challenging physical goals such as achieving 20 pull-ups when you can only do one or the intangibles such as changing the culture of an entire organization.

If you never relent and can continue to endure, you will either die or win. Since the human body and spirit is capable of far beyond what most minds are willing to comprehend, you are unlikely to die.

Once you know what your current mission in life is, endurance is required to reach it.

Influencing people to achieve a goal requires an immense amount of endurance. Face it; people can be frustrating. The weaker the person, the more time they will demand of us. Those without a growing endurance quickly get sucked into fits of frustration and move their gaze away from what's important into the things that don't matter.

Endurance can and should be built, starting with your physical endurance.

If you have the ability to ignore the mental failings telling you to stop running, you have the ability to ignore petty things and go after what's important. In order to even reach that which is important, you have to be able to endure the tiny without it taking you down.

People must know that you "can handle it" for them to follow you. People don't follow those who are weak because weak people can barely help themselves, let alone someone else.

When you have endurance...

You get more chances than other people. You never seem to truly lose, and one thing after another comes your way. Having endurance allows you to endure many things, which in-it-of-itself, will earn you influence with others. If you can outlast the problems that people have, people will know that you are worth following. If anything, why else would one be willing to endure with so much?

CHAPTER 7

What are Principles

Principles are natural laws that govern the interaction with all humans. Principles are core to one's character and core to improvement and interconnection, in reality. These universally accepted rules transcend cultural differences and penetrate deep into what makes all humans human.

While principles can look similar to values, principles are not values. However, values are not principles.

Principles set the grounds for interactions and understanding. One example is trust.

People only trust others who are trustworthy. Trustworthy comes from honesty, doing what you say you will do, and showing up when it matters. A person cannot be trusted without having done these deeds; therefore, in order to obtain trust, one must follow the principles of trust.

Even crooked men will tell you they only trust those who cheat and steal. Yet what they are actually telling you is they trust those people who do what *they expect.* **That is the principle to trust.**

By adopting the use of principles, we have the ability to earn what we want from others. *By adopting the use of principles, we have the ability to earn what we want in ourselves.*

The adoption and use of principles are core to a
leader's character and how a leader's character
performs in the actual real world.

The Marine Corps Leadership Principles

The following is a list of principles that empower and supercharge leadership. By adopting and utilizing the following principles, people will have no doubt that you are a leader and that you ought to be followed. The reason for this is because, in order to be *a person who earns influence from others,* the adoption of these principles in some form is required. These are the principles required for another person to yield influence over themselves to you.

Note: All of these leadership principles are
important, none more important than the other.

Do not let the name "Marine Corps Leadership Principles" fool you. While these principles are useful in war, they are useful in all areas of life where influencing others to compel action is necessary.

Study this list. Know this list. Employ this list.

Know Yourself and
Seek Self Improvement

A leader is constantly seeking to understand where they are personally and looking for how they ought to improve. Those who know themselves maximize their strengths, delegate their weaknesses, and can provide a consistent being. This allows room for other people who may then fill in their strengths and weaknesses into the picture.

The process of discovering and ultimately accepting one's strengths and weaknesses illuminates the path to improvement. The continual improvement of strengths allows one to hone and sharpen their knowledge of self while avoiding wasting time on weaknesses.

Leaders delegate areas of weakness.

Those who know themselves and are improving have additional capacity to understand and deal with others.

> Leaders that follow this principle earn growth both
> in themselves and others.

Be Technically and Tactically Proficient

Every leader must be competent in *their* job. People only follow those who are competent. In order to lead strong people, you must display undeniable competence in the area of your leadership.

Leaders who are not technically proficient are not capable of maintaining the respect of others. People who are not technically proficient often try to "talk the talk" with people who are, but with every statement, they lose influence.

People, especially about technical topics, can tell if you know what you are talking about or not.

For those who struggle to know technical topics, instead of trying to figure out how to appear to be more knowledgeable, just be more knowledgeable. Apply the skills.

A leader does not need to be the best; in fact, that often limits the growth of others, yet they need to be competent in the crafts enough to know how to speak with people to steer the ship.

Leaders that follow this principle earn
the ability to be listened to since their
knowledge can be trusted.

Know Your People and Look Out for Their Welfare

Leadership requires other people. In order to keep people around and make sure they can make the journey with you, it requires that someone know what is going on with them personally and professionally. Those who yield themselves over to you require that you keep their best interest into account.

For those who have not influenced compelled action or have done so without realizing that they are a leader, may not understand the importance of this principle. People can and will lose themselves in what they believe they are supposed to do, often over-exerting themselves and putting everything they have into what they have been asked to do. This is a benefit to your cause but a detriment to the person.

The sustainment of activity over the long term requires that leadership take ownership of all aspects of their cause, including how people are impacted outside your direct influence. This statement should not be read as a mandate to control everything you will lose, but rather that you *will* have to deal with unexpected impacts that your people will get involved in under the direction of yourself and other leadership. It is common for those in leadership positions to fall back to the position that "every person is responsible for themselves", yet those that say this fail to take into account that the person would not be there doing what they're doing if it were not for their influence.

The welfare and best interest of people is a mandate for using leadership.

> Leaders that follow this principle earn
> loyalty while gaining the ability to ask for
> more. This causes others to have greater
> endurance and higher courage.

Keep Your Personnel Informed

The better informed your people are, the less effect uncertainty will have on them. As a result, people are more efficient while they will work, they will possess a better morale and will be better stewards of the greater purpose.

Leaders who keep personnel informed can step back and allow activities and duties to be carried out without them being there to direct every aspect.

Consider for a moment the smartphone and internet. By the year 2020, it has been undeniably proven that humans find information highly valuable as more information has been created and consumed in the last ten years than all of human history combined.

While people can and do drown in information, particularly if it is taken out of an appropriate context, there is never enough information and knowledge about the efforts they support and want to see move forward.

> Following this principle builds a leaders' integrity
> and dependability. These actions cause the entire
> organization to become one.

Set the Example

Setting an example for others is core to leadership. Leadership is about influencing others into action. The first step towards that action is by someone, namely a leader, doing the action first. Leadership, the act of influencing others, literally requires setting an example.

People can and will adopt the same behaviors as you. Sometimes they'll adopt the behavior from your words, but they will truly pick things up by what you do.

The most subtle but most powerful impact you can have on others is to just do something intentional.

If a leader decides that they are seeing incompetence, lack of courage, and lack of integrity in those around them, a leader has but one choice. A leader must start displaying competence, courage, and integrity in order to compel it from others.

> Leaders who follow this principle earn the ability to shape others in the form necessary to achieve the purpose of their leadership.

Ensure That the Task Is Understood, Supervised, and Accomplished

As one scales their leadership, it becomes much more apparent the roles for getting work accomplished. When a leader is leading a small outfit, they often fail to take into consideration the role that they play within the team. As their leadership increases, these roles can be forgotten, leading to collapse.

In the business community, made famous by the book *The E Myth*, all work requires a "technician", a "manager", and an "entrepreneur".

The **"technician"** is the doer. They do the actual technical work. Their focus is *now*.

The **"manager"** is the person who ensures that the processes stay consistent and the work is within expected specifications. Their focus is *the past*.

The **"entrepreneur"** is the person responsible for the overall success of the system and continually looks ahead while shifting and changing the system so it survives. Their focus is *the future*.

Note: In this comparison, *the* leader is most equivalent to the entrepreneur, although a leader can and should be, if at all possible, at all levels.

To achieve success in any organized endeavor, it requires all three of these people to work together even though what they do contradicts each other's individual desires.

It is a leader's job to give clear and concise directions so that the technicians know what they are working on, and the managers have the ability to supervise and ensure that the desired work is getting accomplished.

And yet, communicating this can be more difficult than you are aware.

Tasking others, especially in complex endeavors, requires a leader to improve the communication skills of *everyone* involved, including themselves. There is nothing like tasking a person, them telling you they understand, and then they proceed to do work that has no benefit or is counterproductive. This is painful to everyone involved.

Earning the skill of listening (described in detail later) and teaching others this skill solves this problem.

Leaders who follow this principle bring
effectiveness to what they are organizing.

Train Your Subordinates as a Team

A leader leads many people. These people have all different shapes, sizes, and interests. Yet, in order for them to effectively work *together*, they must *become* a team.

Turning a bunch of individuals into a team requires intentional effort, and the best way to do that is by training them together. By training together, people really become accustomed to each other's strengths and weaknesses. Organically, rather than planned, they can build connections of value.

It is not a leader's job to define every task and personally supervise what is accomplished. It's a leaders' job to hold the vision for the future ahead and build the people who will make that vision possible. *The people* must become a team that chooses to work together, rather than be told they must.

Leaders who follow this principle brings
harmony, enthusiasm, and effectiveness to those
within the organization.

Make Sound and Timely Decisions

The most pressing and valuable resource is time.

Every single decision has to be made with time being a factor. Time impacts how long people can collect information, how long it can be analyzed, and how long it takes for you to act on it. The larger the organization, the more disrupted it is to the amount of time wasted in waiting for decisions to be made.

In general, most people wait too long on the important decisions and take too long on the trivial ones.

Many leaders recommend making decisions somewhere between having 60% to 80% of the data available to make the decision. While it is uncomfortable to make decisions with 20–40% of uncertainty, the time it takes to get the remaining information without "moving forward" scales non-linearly and thus takes too long and is impractical to find. Put in other words, each 1% increase in information finding takes continually more than 1 unit of work.

It isn't until a decision is made and actions begins does the world reveal the remaining information.

It is impossible to predict the world and all its complexities. The only way to master it is by maneuvering through it, changing and weaving as new information presents itself.

> Leaders who follow this principle will grow
> in intuition, move quickly and efficiently,
> and have the best chance of staying ahead
> of the problems ahead.

Develop a Sense of Responsibility Among Your Subordinates

There is a reason why the US military always organizes every unit into three sections, whether it is a small fire team or a brigade. **A leader quickly finds out that it is difficult to manage more than three people effectively.** The only way to overcome this problem is through developing leadership and ownership in those beneath you.

Scale and big impact are *only* possible when *other* people take ownership and execute the overall plan. This requires building trust, confidence, and respect with others.

Even within small teams of three or four, it becomes apparent just how much getting anything done requires yielding over ownership.

The best working teams completely depend upon the owned work of others.

A few ways to build on this principle are delegating effectively, training, and mentoring others to own the purpose of leadership.

Leaders who follow this principle create
the possibility of a larger and more resilient
organization by subordinates owning the future.

Employ Your Command within its Capabilities

Not only must you know yourself and know others, but you must also know the organization as a *whole*. Paying attention to how the team operates as a team will determine your ability to know if tasking the team will cause struggle or be accomplished with ease.

It is important to know the breaking point of your team, so when the time is right, you will know how far you can push the team to maximize opportunities.

- You must be willing to challenge them.
- You must be willing to be wrong.
- You must be willing to push too far.

When a team is pushed almost to breaking and then succeeds, those who did not believe will become believers. Those who did not believe that they personally could do it will become advocates for what is possible the next time around.

Operating on less than 80% of what is capable creates boredom and a drifting mind. Operating at 90% creates awareness and effective action. Operating at 100% for longer than a very short duration inevitably creates collapse. However, when the time is right, the team will utilize their past experiences, rise to the occasion and operate greater than 100% of capability.

Leaders who follow this principle create growth,
trust, and mutual respect.

Seek Responsibilities and Take Responsibility

Actively seeking out responsibility is the opposite of easy and what is expected. Most people are unwilling to raise their hand to volunteer because success and failure falls squarely on them.

However, this is the only way to grow and steer the future.

Leadership is imbued with responsibility. Leaders are responsible for the destination of everyone. Leaders are responsible for the welfare of those that are brought along on your journey. Leaders are responsible for everything that happens in-between.

By seeking responsibilities and taking them, it continually prepares us mentally and physically to deal with the world as it is. Every responsibility taken reduces reliance upon excuses, replacing them with ownership and an aware mind.

Remember what is learned by leaders setting an example. Taking responsibility ourselves starts to cause others to take responsibilities as well.

Just remember that when a person who newly takes up responsibility for something bad that happens, instead of punishing them, give hearty praise.

Leaders who follow this principle create
bearing, integrity, tact, courage, endurance, and
dependability in others. Responsibility creates a
culture of ownership.

CHAPTER 8

Strategies and Tactics for Building Your Character

This section contains strategies and tactics that I personally know work. Although these have worked for me, you should become diverse and creative in this growth endeavor. The effort of taking multiple approaches will make you well versed in the aspects of your desired character improvements.

Overall, I recommend a healthy *lifelong* pursuit of character growth.

Positive character growth is not automatic. What I can tell you is it appears that the older a person is, the less likely they desire to improve themselves, especially if they haven't had a lifelong desire for improvement. This doesn't mean that older people cannot improve, but you can see that older folks often get **caught up in their own personal stories** about why they cannot, excuses, and become difficult to move. These stories act as cement that slowly glues them into a stiff and rigid person, never letting them move forward. But this doesn't have to be you.

The truth is they can improve, and you definitely can too.

Carry Information on You to Study

My recommendations are to bring 3x5 or flashcards on you that contain the character-building information that you are looking to ingrain more. What will happen as you look at them and study them throughout the day, you are training yourself to apply those when you come into contact with different circumstances that require those.

Some recommendations:

- List of Marine Corps Leadership Traits and Principles
- Individual traits or principles
- Small actions to be performed throughout the day
- Small messages to yourself
- Personal goals

Do Something That You Receive No Material Benefit

Volunteer somewhere, go out of your way to open the door for someone, just do anything that does not actually provide you with a benefit.

Note: This isn't about making your character altruistic. This is about breaking habits and patterns of thinking. You need to focus on other people's needs, so you can *identify* what they are and learn how to provide value, **as a leader does.**

If possible, attempt to volunteer at an organization to help them deal with the "bigger" problems, such as managing their affairs. I recommend looking for board work, leadership roles, etc.

Begin Reflecting and Acting on the Results

If you don't already spend some time each week reflecting on how your week went, then consider starting. This is a perfect opportunity to identify what you said you were going to do but didn't. To break down the poor character outbursts that you had and then seeking to rectify them.

I recommend writing out as many poor character actions that you performed and how you'll perform next time those situations come up.

If you get frustrated easily, you need to work that out of your system. Something about the way you're interacting with the world is causing yourself stress that you shouldn't have.

Everyone gets frustrated for sure, but the people who are NOT practicing and using influence to lead people will get influenced over silly things. They have control issues. They say "can't" often.

If you *really believe* that you can influence and lead people, it's only a matter of time until you've tackled nearly every problem you set yourself on.

Sooner or later, you will run into the problem that most things are not worth your attention.

Challenge Yourself Physically and Mentally

People today complain about testing. They don't want to be evaluated and don't want to be measured against anything. Yet, internalize the fact that challenges bring growth; you should seek to challenge yourself.

Challenging yourself physically, for example, will pay off in many different ways. As mentioned before about endurance, if you are capable of physically traveling long distances, you will have a greater ability to handle the small stresses that bother others. The more you can challenge yourself, the more you will find that other people's challenges are easy.

Why this is important is that your growth will allow you to assist others with their issues at higher and higher levels. Growth is a necessary requirement for having the privilege of tackling larger and larger issues. And this growth only comes from challenging yourself.

Can you do 50 pushups? What about 100?

How about 20 pullups? Or even just 5?

Can you run 3 miles in less than 20 minutes? Can you run 3 miles at all?

Can you handle high emotions being thrown at you without your body believing you are in danger?

Can you communicate when you are frustrated without frustrating others?

These are definite challenges for most people, and yet solving these problems goes a very, *very* long way. Those who have tackled these challenges, maybe even a lifetime ago, ought to look for *new and different* challenges that are appropriate for the point in life where they are at.

One of the great mysteries in life is how difficult it is for us to see interconnections that are not obvious.

We fail to make the connection between how your morning starts and how it helps determine how your day goes. Awareness, awareness, awareness.

Constantly Seek out Purpose and Meaning

While purpose and meaning are discussed in depth further in this book, there is a peculiar side effect of seeking out purpose. You begin to see people from a different light than you did before. As you discover purpose and understanding of the world, you ought to develop a more complex relationship with the realities that you face.

One example is the unique quirks of people. Quirks can be discovered in people you have known for a long time, yet you never noticed them until you did. If a person's quirks could jeopardize an initiative that is going on, it might make sense to redeploy them into another position where they can aid rather than detract.

The act of seeking out purpose and meaning will pull you back and disconnect from the meanings that "they" impart on you and instead give you the power to see what "*is.*"

Doing this act changes your physiological state, giving you breathing room not to react, instead giving you a chance to **choose** what to do rather than doing the automatic response.

> Clarity of choice is the result of finding
> purpose and meaning.

Internalize Being Invulnerable

"Nothing you do will matter in the cosmos of time."
—Dan Peña.

An entire book could be written about the topic of cultivating the sense of being invulnerable, but the topic will be condensed down to the most relevant points.

It is often necessary and helpful to meet the challenges in life by thinking of yourself as invulnerable. In most situations, accept that no words can harm you and that even physical harm may not hurt you like you think it could. Even physical harm can empower you. It is often necessary in life to acknowledge that things are going to be OK and give yourself enough credit and leeway for being able to handle what comes.

When you receive criticism, instead of becoming defensive, take a step back and consider what it *really* means about you and the other person.

And yet, sometimes it's necessary to become vulnerable.

When you are with a friend sharing personal feelings, allow yourself to be present rather than focused on what you think or feel. When it's necessary to think about the needs of others, become a fleshy person so you can understand others and provide for their needs. Not only does this earn influence with them greatly, but it also helps *them* solve their own problems.

> Outside of the areas of having concern for
> the wellbeing of others, raise your level of
> concerns, and lose your fear.

Internalize the following true facts:

- Nothing you will ever do will matter on a long enough scale.
- You're going to die, you don't know when, and you don't really get to choose.
- When you die, you'll soon be forgotten, permanently.
- Control is only a feeling. You are *not* in control. **Nobody is in control.**

Everyone you know, have ever known, or have ever heard of is bound by the same reality whether they accept it or not. They will accept it or not. We will.

You may be wondering, if these aspects are true, what matters then?

It matters what you do *now*. The results *can* matter for a long enough time to be worth aiming towards, and you *can* influence the direction where change occurs.

This is not possible to those who spend their days fearful of their lives, fearful they won't make an impact, and fearful that they cannot control other people.

Reader: If you're reading this in safety away from a world filled with war, you're living in one of the greatest times in human history.

This is the time to be building *long* and building *big*. The times of great peace and plenty are the times to invest rather than the time to be fearful. Fearful may feel like it prevents you from dying, but it also prevents you from doing the activities that matter at the opportune times.

The following sections outline the core of what it means to internalize invulnerability:

There is no Long a Reason to Become Defensive

The common use of the phrase "being defensive" means that you *feel* the physiological *feelings* of fear. It is the behavior that somehow you or others will be minimized or eliminated, and you better do something, or you'll no longer exist.

FALSE.

This situation is most observable when people get into verbal discussions. Sure, you might know the "truth" and feel the need to let truth have its day. But if you take a step back and look at what's really going on, you are fearful.

Examine the following Nietzsche quote on those who try to stand tall for "truth":

> *Of suffering "for the truth's sake"! even in your own defense! It spoils all the innocence and fine neutrality of your conscience; it makes you headstrong against objections and red rags; it stupefies, animalizes, and brutalizes, when in the struggle with danger, slander, suspicion, expulsion, and even worse*

consequences of enmity, ye have at last to play your last card as
protectors of truth upon earth--as though "the Truth" were such
an innocent and incompetent creature as to require protectors!
—Friedrich Nietzsche in *Beyond Good and Evil*

If every value you feel ***needs*** defending is so universally true and valuable, shouldn't it be self-evident to others from the actions displayed from holding these values?

In other words, shouldn't good and great values prevail and be understood without you needing to go to war over them?

If you accept this premise, still know that **there will be people who still don't get it.** Consider whether such as a person is worth lowering yourself to get aggressive and upset.

Instead of *you* becoming defensive, consider the other side.

Think about how the other person feels. Consider for a moment that if the other person is becoming heated and defensive, what does it say about the situation? ***You have created conditions where the other person is fearful.*** Some aspect of their belief system is now in question and is being challenged (at least in their mind). If it comes from what you are saying, if you are intending on your idea being "dominate", doesn't their defensive actions already indicate that you have won?

Why on earth would *you* feel the need to become defensive?

Influencing from the frustration of others

Let's put aside hypothetical heated conversations you might fall into for the moment. When others come to you in frustration, you should understand something important. They are not frustrated at you, even if it makes logical sense to be.

These people are stuck with the *feeling* of frustration.

Frustration is a *feeling*. It ought not to be reasoned with nor explained away. It is a real physiological feeling that, in fact, feels terrible. So terrible that it will cause people to vent their frustrations in an unbelievable number of ways.

Frustration is the feeling that things are no longer moving forward as they "ought to", and the person in front of you feels that.

In most cases, when people come to you with frustration, they are seeking to remove this affliction, and they've chosen you. **If you are not aware of what is going on, you may get sucked into their feelings and become defensive. If you do that, you will lose the opportunity to earn influence by being present.**

You have a choice. Earn influence, grow and gain in your life or "defend yourself", lose influence with others and go nowhere.

These opportunities present themselves to those who have internalized they are invulnerable.

Become Invulnerable by Holding Nothing Back

When we are *vulnerable,* we limit ourselves on what we are willing to do. Vulnerable people are overly sensitive to the cares and sensitivities of others and, in turn, are sensitive themselves to what others do. While it's important to gain the ability to be *intentionally* sensitive to others' concerns, those who are sensitive cannot be followed into difficult places.

In other words, sensitive people, by their nature, are not resilient and are difficult to work with, *let alone be positively influenced by them.*

Understand at times; *absolutely everything* will be standing in the way of you leading to the ends you are intending, even yourself. Leaders need the endurance to withstand small issues without becoming bitter, the tact to politely sidestep triviality and time-wasters, and the courage to say to the point direct statements without the fear of loss.

This is why cultivating character is vitally important.

Holding nothing back does not mean going too far. When people go too far, they are fearful that they will not be able to reach the end without going in excess. This isn't dedication to the mission at hand; it's fear driving decision-making.

Invulnerability is cultivated when we stay focused on the ends and doing everything that is necessary to get *there* but not further.

Stay Focused on Earning Influence and Spending it Smartly

The easiest way to build invulnerability is staying focused on earning influence. Absolutely every moment of the day, any interaction with a person, can earn you influence if you see these opportunities.

Consider for a moment that you are receiving a gift because of something you've done. On one hand, you could be excited that someone cares about you. (It feels good after all!) But know, depending on how you accept it, know this is spending influence purely by accepting it.

In this situation, instead, consider having **extreme bashful grace** and reward the person by highlighting that they possess such admirable qualities of care and concern for others. The more that you see this as an opportunity to **reward them,** the more you'll actually earn.

> Leaders who reduce their need for
> validation can raise others much higher than
> they can by themselves.

This is *only possible* for those who keep their eyes on earning influence and moving forward with people. These actions build invulnerability because every action you turn around weans you off the need for external validation.

Those who know where they are going, and aim right, know whether or not their actions are valid or not. Praise from others ought not be needed.

If you find yourself needing praise for your actions, consider whether or not you'd praise yourself.

Drop All Harbored Negative Emotions

If there has been anything in the past that has caused you negative emotions, consider ending your attachment to it. Negative emotions harbored overtime sap our abilities to become invulnerable and make us less able to stay focused.

Given it is often our bad experiences with people that create harbored negative emotions, the easiest ways to drop the negativity is through forgiveness, acceptance, and apologizing.

Influence Tip: Apologize to Fix Relationships

One of the easiest ways to fix relationships is to apologize. It is nearly impossible for a relationship not to amend at least a little bit if you apologize, even if there is not much to apologize for. This may seem strange but doing so indicates to the person by your behavior that you are considerate for them, disproving what they may have thought before. After leaving that experience, it opens up the relationship to exist beyond animosity.

Internalize you are invulnerable, and you will
be able to focus on empowering others to help
achieve purposeful ends.

Earn Influence with Others

Consistently and Strategically

> *"You can make more friends in two months by becoming*
> *interested in other people than you can in two years*
> *by trying to get other people interested in you."*
>
> —Dale Carnegie, *How to Win Friends and Influence People*

Before we get into the depths of how to earn influence with others, we ought to solidify our understand of **why** we will go through the effort to earn influence and how influence plays an integral part in what we are trying to achieve.

The purpose of growing influence is to direct the results of it towards something bigger than our individual selves.

This is how communities are started. This is how humanity advances. This is how people survive. **Influence, it turns out, is serious business.**

This is how we hold together our tribes without people falling into the cracks. This is how individual decay is prevented and reversed. This is achieved by reaching out to people, looking them in the eye, getting to know their concerns and desires, and then influencing them to take action. These are the unglamorous actions that actually make things happen, yet these activities often happen behind the scenes.

Let's Not Forget Influence *is* Real

It seems silly to say the following statement: however, it's necessary. **The phenomenon of influence is *actually* real**. People *willingly* yield over power to others, and the reason they're willing to do it is because they *believe* they'll benefit as a result.

CHAPTER 9

Influence is Serious Business

Influence isn't a made-up system or a game but a distinctly natural process. Possessing the ability to lead people does not come from a matrix of rules written by bureaucratic government lawyers. It exists, irrespective of culture, societies, or empires. **People either *follow you*, or they *don't*. They do this entirely in response to what YOU do to earn it.**

"Bad" people would like us to believe that influence is gained through force. By making people afraid that something bad will happen to them if they don't. Those that believe this have not been connected with a leader. Instead, they are outsiders looking in and guessing at how it "must" work.

You should know by now that a person who thinks influence is gained through force is crooked in their character and following their advice will make you crooked in yours.

Yes, utilizing fear can get people to move towards and complete an activity; however, only as long as you are there to project the fear. And yet, only for so long.

There is another way.

Influence Sort of Works Like Money

To create an example, imagine that influence is similar to money. Everyone has an influence account with others. In order to spend it, you have to fill it up first. And like any account, the more you fill it up, the more you can spend at one time. **If you want to grow your influence**, like money, you want to increase your rate of income compared to the increase in your expenses.

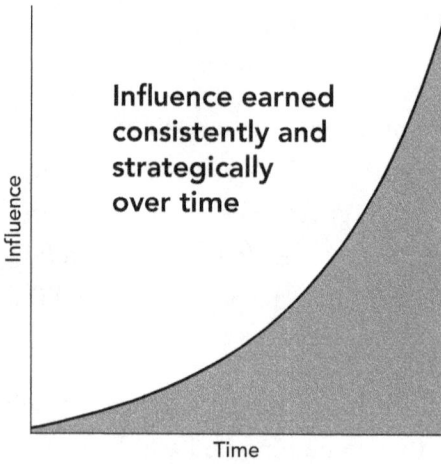

On the left, you can see two charts. The chart on the top left is what it looks like to continually earn influence and to earn it with strategy. The bottom left chart is the same, but with influence spent in red.

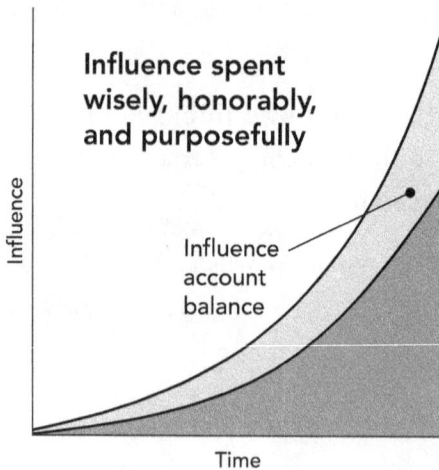

You can see in these charts that the influence spent (in dark gray) will never outgrow the influence earned (in light gray). As time goes on, more influence is accrued, allowing for greater compelling of action.

In order to get people to take bigger actions, more influence has to be earned at a continuous and larger rate than what is spent.

Influence earned, but spent poorly and too often.

Backfires and relationship
tensions due to overspending

Influence

Time

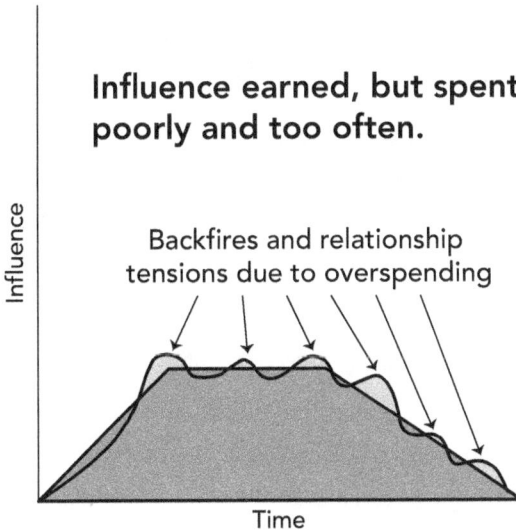

However, note the picture above. When influence is not earned well and influence is spent too often and poorly, it results in overspending. When influence is overspent, it causes chaotic flare-ups in the relationship and will ultimately end influence with the other person.

Leadership influence is *earned*.

Positive influence from others is *earned consistently* over time. And obtaining higher levels of it is *earned* through *strategic actions*. Ideally, the majority of actions that you take earns influence.

There Are Many Different Ways to Earn Influence

Some methods of earning influence work with all people and others will only work with certain individuals.

One such example is a friend who earns influence with his wife by cleaning the table and putting away the dishes. If he does any other cleaning activities, he earns little influence. But if he does the few things that his wife *really wants*, she becomes a completely different person. Seemingly, unlocked.

Warning: Avoid Temptations for Enrichment. You'll Go Broke

As you put other people in the position where they feel the need to serve you, you will start finding yourself on the receiving end. People will start doing things for you, seemingly out of nowhere. Creating a culture of giving and positive influence can do this. This brings about dangers for leadership.

If you take goods and services by those you've influenced, *you are spending influence.* If every time you earn a little, you spend a little, you'll never be able to spend a lot. It is imperative that you train your mind, body, and spirit to see that the end state and the goals you seek are far larger and more important than anything they can give you.

Trust me.

To reach your goals, you will need to spend *a lot*. You do not want to go about blindly spending. Let me show you what I know about earning, and give your ideas about how to spend it.

Influence Tip: Take Caution with Receiving Gifts

If you receive gifts for things that you have done, understand it for what it is; a person who is put in a position of unbalanced influence. Accept low-value gifts gracefully, turn away expensive ones, and stay your course.

CHAPTER 10

Influence is Earned by Performing Actions for Others

Now that we know that leadership is influence and that our personal character is so valuable, and there is an influence balance that we need to build so we can spend it, we now need to get to the business of earning influence.

You should have realized by now that influence is earned by performing actions. These actions need to be performed in front of others, either in service for them or for them to physically see in order to influence them (and others whom they tell). What these actions are, how they look, and when you do them is part of the art and mastery of leadership.

Sometimes the actions are physical, such as you helping to carry someone's couch. Other times it is just being present while someone shares their feelings. Sometimes it's being asked to take care of something that another person is having a hard time with. And even other times, it is emoting emotions that help a person get energized and motivated to get off their butt and move in the direction they really feel they ought to but are not.

For every person earning influence will be different. This is precisely why there are different "leadership styles."

Influence Tip: Influence with Clothes

Even wearing nice clothes can earn you influence. In many strange ways, the clothes that you wear sets the nature of your relationship with other people. You might notice how wearing different clothes might make you feel. Not because of the material, but the nature of the looks. For some, the thought of wearing a monk robe or a business suit and then going out into public, makes them feel uncomfortable. This is a clear sign that you receive feelings just from the clothes themselves. Consider for a moment that others have physical effects as well. When you wear certain clothes in public, it dramatically elevates you out of the common crowd. However, keep in mind, once you are visible in public you ought to be on your absolute best behavior. A well or uniquely dressed person acting nasty in public draws **long-term negative emotions from others.**

Influence earned is not just from action. It is action recognized.

Something to keep in mind is these actions have to be recognized by those people you are trying to influence. They must be the recipient of the actions, or they must have seen or heard about the actions performed. Just as in "sales", if the person doesn't value what actions you have done, then no influence is earned. Earning influence requires getting to know the person.

Your actions should show that you have concern for them personally.

Interactions you have with others should continually show that you have concern for their needs and values, which is why it's important to cultivate having your head in the right place. **Character matters.**

Just as an example, if you are part of an organization and if you don't believe that others are providing value, you will act that way. Your actions will suck all the oxygen out of the room and get all the attention pointed your way. **If you believe other people are providing value and can provide more value,** you will consistently and constantly let them know that what they do, is going to bring them to victory and that by reaching the next level, the team will be able to reach the goals quicker.

It is imperative that you cultivate a mindset for developing and growing success by seeking out what others are doing well and determining how you can help the process of them moving forward with greater impact.

Do continuous actions because you're not always going to know which actions will have the greatest impact.

Maybe it was a speech you did. Maybe it's when you put your arm around their shoulder and listened. Maybe it was asking about how their cat is doing. You may never know ahead of time what actions will have unspeakably large impacts.

This is why **continuous actions** *are so important.*

Continuous diverse actions will allow you to try different techniques and eventually find out "what does this person really value?" It is likely that you will not know consciously what actions will have the largest effect. For every person, it's different.

Kind actions, even small ones, can be remembered for a lifetime.

You might be wondering, "How will I have time to impact everyone?"

Consistent small actions, while important for maintaining and continually earning, are only one-half of the picture. The other side of the coin is earning **strategically**. This is where strategic actions play a role.

> Strategy is a series of planned actions that are designed to achieve large goals.

Conscious leaders are intentional. Leaders are consciously aware of where they are trying to go and that they are bringing "the people" with them. In order to do that, you must practice strategy to get there. Even if you have never built and executed a strategy before, you can.

Let's Damper A Bit of Idealism

While "doing good" is peppered throughout this text, especially as it relates to earning influence, do not assume that everything in leadership is sunshine and rainbows. In order for people to reach their fullest potential, they must often go through considerably challenging experiences that frustrate and test one's resolve.

If a leader is doing their job, there will be instances where the relationship will feel strained. This is the cost of achieving a vision.

Consider for a moment what it might take to compel someone to do the dirtiest and toughest jobs? How about getting a person to enact judgement and justice?

There are Many Ways to Earn Influence

Before we get into depth on earning influence through any particular strategy or series of tactics, let's just look at a list of tactics that can be used at any time.

All of the following earn influence.

Not only do they work and work well, but they are also easy to do. Use them, and pepper them throughout your life.

1. Boosting someone's worth and value through praise. Especially in public.

2. Doing something for them physically. Such as helping lift a load.

3. Write a handwritten note, showing them you "care", and think about them.

4. Showing someone that some "crazy" task is well within the realm of possibility. *There is an unbelievable number of mini-micro-easy tasks that people think are nearly impossible.*

5. Remind someone of something good they have done. Small or large.

CHAPTER 11

Skills for Earning Influence

The following chapters are the skills that are critical for earning influence. Each of these activities will *immediately* set you apart from others as a leader. Make no mistake that these skills are easy to "understand" but require consistent application in order to improve.

At some point, these skills are likely to become second nature; however, **even still,** the conscious, consistent application of them is required for improvement.

CHAPTER 12

Asking Questions

You only get the answers to the questions you ask.

Asking questions is the most important and powerful skill that you can develop, especially in the pursuit of earning influence.

Asking questions is the act of finding out the truth about anything and setting the trajectory for the next actions to come.

Questions, and the act of asking them, have powerful, far-reaching effects beyond just what meets the eye.

Asking questions has the power to...

- Change the trajectory of lives.
- Discover great opportunities while avoiding distractions.
- Collecting the right information, at the right time, for the right reasons.
- Break patterns of thinking and behavior.
- Earn influence continually and strategically.
- Spend influence wisely and purposefully.

Questions and Questioning Are Different

We must remain crystal clear on the task of asking questions. Questioning is different than asking questions. Questioning is an act of distrust and putting someone in the grilling seat. I am not saying there is no value in questioning but given that questioning is an act of **fear and force,** it can be a **toxic way to spend influence.** It is possible to earn influence while questioning someone; however, it should be used with caution.

People who ask questions are genuinely looking for ideas from the other person. Just by asking questions of others, it shows you value them. It says that you aren't sure of something, and you believe they can help you **because they can.**

By putting yourself in a position of not knowing and then empowering the person to provide answers, it raises them to a higher position.

Quality Questions Are Required for Building Knowledge and Earning Influence

Questions are the lifeblood of knowledge and core to developing strategic influence with individuals. How do you know anything about another person if you don't ask questions?

- What is their favorite food?
- What is the name of their children?
- Will they accept [insert idea] if I ask them?

If You Don't Ask, You Rely on Randomness

Questions are critical to acquiring knowledge. As a reminder, Knowledge is not information. Information is facts and factoids that come across your various sensors (hear, see, smell, etc.). Knowledge is a deeper understanding that strings together information with experience.

Questions are the primary methodology for choosing what information is presented to us, the order that we need.

Your Questions State Where You Are

If you cannot imagine the question, you cannot conceive the answer. If you cannot ask the question, you cannot receive an answer. And lastly, if you cannot ask higher-level questions, you cannot receive higher-level answers.

This isn't to say that when you come across people and listen to what they have to say that you cannot take in "the answer." But simply because you haven't imagined or formulated a question, you will have a difficult time internalizing the meaning of someone's statements.

When you speak with a "higher level" person, they often give high-level statements. Without leveling up your ability to ask questions, this potential resource will remain locked. **This is why making statements to a "higher level" person is a waste of your time. Ask questions!!!**

Questions give you insight into OTHERS

Just like your questions say much about you, the answers will say much about the person who is answering. Good questions will yield results that will tell you if you are driving too hard or if you need to begin driving harder.

Questions have the potential to let you know the hidden capabilities of people who might not have enough confidence to act out certain behaviors in public that the person really ought to. One such example is a person who may be very skilled at drawing but instead spends their time selling. Acknowledging someone's desires to do other tasks is a way to earn influence.

Questions have the ability to provide some information for ascertaining the truth and determining what is really going on. It is rarely the case, unless you make a culture out of it, that you will get the full truth when you ask questions. However, asking questions will allow you to start to gain further insight into what you might need to do.

By doing this, you have the potential to earn influence by doing the **right** action that people are waiting on you to perform but just aren't really saying it out loud.

> Make no mistake; people are waiting for someone, perhaps you, to take action on something right now.

How to Earn Influence with Questions

Asking questions is a highly effective form of earning influence. As part of an earning influence continually, it is a wise idea to form the habit of asking questions of people continually. Questions, especially simple ones, have the ability to earn considerable influence with others. In many cases, questions earn you enough influence to get your foot in the door and will allow you to perform larger actions to earn even more.

Questions show that you are interested in the other person.

By showing interest in another person, it gives them life and lifts them up. This will make people always want to come to you, even if you do this only a little bit. As people get older, they become more focused on what they have going on themselves and end up showing very little interest in others. This gives you room to earn this influence.

Questions allow you to show empathy.

The skill of empathy is described in depth below, so the only statement that is needed is that questions are very helpful for employing the skill of empathy. Use it.

Questions are useful for mentoring others into new areas of thinking.

By bringing others into areas they had not considered before, it gives them new space to think about what's possible. They will grow, and you will have been the reason.

Questions are a method of how YOU get truly heard

If you analyze conversations well enough, you will that people talk past each other. They may converse on the same topic, but their statements just sit on top of each other but never really intersect and connect.

When you ask questions, such as clarification about what a person has said, you begin to deeply connect with what the other person is saying. If you ask a couple of questions about them, it opens up space for them to listen to what you have to say. In fact, by asking questions, you have already prompted them a few times to start paying attention to you when you state your point.

Four Ways to Ask Great Questions

The return on asking questions spans from negligible to great. It is not until you ask great questions will truly see the value of asking questions. Great questions are like missing keys that unlock what is truly beneath the surface.

1. Ask direct questions that get straight to the point.

Instead of beating around the bush, if you ask good direct questions to people, instead of giving vague and weak answers, they will give you direct, confident information. There is no doubt based on the way you ask the question; it will prompt the other person to return the same. Ask a question weakly, get a weak response.

Asking direct questions earns influence because it gives the other person the ability to "say it like it is" to someone who might be able to use the information.

2. Ask questions that incite emotional replies.

These questions do not play around. They jump deep in and try to break the mold of a person's defenses. By asking questions that pull out emotions, good, bad, or otherwise, you show that you are interested in experiencing the real person.

Asking about a person's family can do it. Asking a person why they do something odd or strange can do it. Asking their opinion about a controversial topic can do it. Even if you handle it poorly by reacting to what they say, you need this experience.

Note: Emotional replies don't come from emotional questions. Do not ask a question in a state of emotions because then you become the centerpiece of the discussion.

Questions that incite emotions earn influence because the other person knows you care about them deep down and can handle their less perfect nature.

3. Ask difficult questions. Ones that you *don't want to ask*, but you *want to know* the answer.

These questions will make you uncomfortable. There are all sorts of questions that we want to ask people, but we **fear** what would happen if we ask them. Well, it turns out that people often want to talk about those topics, but they **fear** that you cannot handle it. This stalemate creates tension that ought to be displaced, creating a better environment of trust and understanding.

Difficult questions earn you influence because the other person learns you can be trusted with difficult situations.

4. Ask open-ended questions.

Open-ended questions get a person to open up about a topic and take it absolutely anywhere they want to go with it. An open-ended question is one that cannot be answered with 1 or 2 words. These questions are not definitive, so a yes or a no should not be possible.

If you really want to know where a person's mind takes them, make sure to avoid any hints or leading information when asking open-ended questions, that way, the other person is in full control from the start.

People will eventually hit the edge where they no longer provide "sensitive" information and require follow-up questions to get to deeper places. Ask follow-up questions to take them further down the rabbit hole.

Open-ended questions earn influence because it shows your infinite interest in them and their ideas.

How to Improve the Skill of Asking Questions

You need to get into the habit of leading with questions. Start as many conversations as you can with a question. This will lead to the habit of asking questions early on in the conversation. Before engaging a person, or early in the engagement, ask yourself, "what questions should I be asking this person?"

In many conversations, shoot for 80% or more of what you say to be questions. Do not be cheeky with this and ask dumb questions just for the sake of increasing numbers. If anything, say less.

Lastly, consider employing the following three questions then reply approach:

"Question, Listen, Question, Listen, Question, Listen and then reply."

Do you really know what listening is? That topic is next…

CHAPTER 13

Listening

Listening is the skill of being able to clearly receive communications from others.

Listening is perhaps the most important skill you can learn to **earn influence continually and strategically.** If you listen well, you *will* earn influence and will help you spend your influence effectively.

Take note; listening is one of the most important points in the book. Really listening, which will be described in a moment, requires a different kind of thinking than what is practiced by most.

What is Listening?

There are two forms of listening (**Passive and Active**), and there are **at least** three different forms of content that is provided by a speaker (**Technical Content, Intent, and Emotional Content**).

Core Definitions

- **Passive Listening** – The act of listening without engaging the speaker.
- **Active Listening** – The act of listening by seeking clarification.
- **Technical Content** – The literal words that a person communicates.
- **Intent** – The exact message that a person is actually *trying* to convey.

- **Emotional Content** – What the person feels, which is driving the desire to communicate.

Passive and Active Listening

Passive listening is the act of listening without engaging with the speaker. Active listening is the act of listening by seeking clarification, most commonly through **questions.** Both forms of listening have strengths and weaknesses.

Passive listening gives you the ability to receive communications with no risk of contamination from you.

Those practicing passive listening allow the other person the space to say whatever it is that they want to say. By giving the floor nearly entirely to the other person, the communication can come out naturally without being coerced or modified by the presence of the listener. Oftentimes, when a listener begins speaking, they modify the trajectory and topic of the original speaker, preventing the person from saying everything they feel they need to say.

As the speaker progresses, the listener *may* inject small questions to help the person clarify what they are saying. These small and innocent questions send a powerful signal to the speaker that someone is very interested in them. **This earns the listener influence.**

If a listener does not ask questions, the listener risks not knowing exactly what is being communicated and may then proceed with faulty assumed information. As one improves in intuition and experience, the balance of interaction can be discovered.

Active listening, on the other hand, gives one the ability to interact with what the speaker is trying to communicate. It is often the case that what people literally say (the technical content) is not what they mean, **exactly**. Without really interacting with the person, the truth stays locked away.

In order to get at what they are really meaning, questions can be deployed that will help them articulate what they desire to communicate. The strengths of this approach should be obvious. By asking questions instead of receiving partially correct or misleading signals, you get to what the person actually wants to be communicated. The weakness is that this approach requires more effort, time and if one performs poorly, it can lead to tangents, "water cooler talk", and completely avoiding what the person wanted to communicate.

Technical Content, Intent, and Emotional Content

There are likely more than just three dimensions to communication, but these three are the most important to know and work with well. Those who fail to get a handle on all three of these communications are likely to misunderstand what is really being communicated, act on trivial rather than critical information, and miss the opportunities to earn influence.

The following sections contain a few tactics for each of these dimensions that help one listen effectively.

How to Listen Effectively

Employ Empathy to Find Emotional Content

People's emotional state is serious business that is under-served and looked over most. A person's emotional state often drives them to perform behaviors that can be detrimental to themselves and others, especially in the case of intense emotions like panic. Emotions require the practice of empathy, which is accurately identifying the emotion a person is experiencing. It turns out, using empathy is a very powerful way to continually earn influence.

In the relationship book "Men are from Mars and Women are from Venus" written by John Gray, it details the importance of understanding what emotions are, what they want, and how to handle them appropriately.

Emotions seek to be expressed, acknowledged, and identified. Emotions seek *nothing else* from a listener.

Unfortunately, people have difficulties identifying what emotional state they are in. This is why a speaker has vibrant elation when someone identifies the emotion.

Instead of saying you care about someone, try helping them understand what emotional state has them ensnared. The way you do that is by identifying, out loud, the emotional state the other person is experiencing.

It's that simple.

The following is a magic sentence that can applied in almost every imaginable situation to both help an emotional speaker and earn influence...

You seem [*insert emotion here*].

Here is the list of core emotional states, ordered roughly by how often you are likely to be experienced:

1. Frustrated   5. Confused
2. Excited   6. Satisfied
3. Concerned   7. Bored
4. Disappointed

Influence Tip: Just try and name it

An important note on employing empathy; avoid focusing too much on getting the emotion right; just try and name it. If the person does not feel the stated emotion, then they will simply correct you. Remember, you are working with them in order to figure out the emotional state, and by being concerned about their emotional state, it proves beyond a shadow of a doubt that you care about them *personally*. The result of which is added influence.

Try to find the intent as quickly as possible.

It is often, but not always, the case that a person has a reason they are coming to talk to you. You need to get to the intent of the communication as quickly as feasible, so the communications can center around what should actually be discussed. This will avoid a significant amount of wasted communications.

In many common scenarios, the person is coming to you because their feelings on a subject have reached a point that they need to be expressed. Sometimes, however, there is a larger point to someone's communications, and it might be worth hearing. This is the "intent" of the communications.

While listening to a person, one should guard themselves against looking at details too quickly at what is being explicitly stated. Many people have a difficult time stating anything other than a long string of specific facts rather than summarizations. Unfortunately for the listener, it is easy to drown and become distracted in facts, just trying to get to the point. Here is one such example:

> "Yesterday, I was at the Jones Library in downtown Covington. I bumped into Mary Ann. Mary Ann works for the Johnson Company, the one I was telling you about last week. Well, anyway, I asked Mary Ann about the Tinko project. She said she had looked at it but won't be able to get back to us for another week. But hey, you know, she said that Mike over in accounting wants to see our proposal too. I don't know Mike, except that he works for Pyramid Inc. I really don't like that company, because when I was working at Quicktec, there were a number of people who contracted there from Pyramid Inc. They're so annoying to work with."

In this near-real example, you might be asking, **"what is the point of this story?"**

Summarizing, it looks like "Mary will not be able to get back with us for another week." This verbose paragraph was nothing more than a simple update. It contained nothing more of interest on the surface.

There are many *many* **many** people who speak like this in the world. Caution, without guidance and steering the conversation through questions, these discussions can and will steal your time.

If you don't get a person to provide you with the point of them talking to you as quickly as possible, you may never know why they are communicating with you in the first place, let alone what you can do with the information provided.

Influence Tip: Getting to the Point

While it may not always be appropriate, one way to get to the point quickly is asking, "**what are you trying to say.**" Especially if the person has made a number of statements that don't seem to really be leading to what would be a "point." Asking this question lets them know, "hey, this person cares what I am saying, but they want to really hear what I'm **trying** to say." It appears that sometimes people have a hard time *finding* the point without being asked...

Guide the flow of Technical Content to get only the details necessary for making decisions.

Technical Content is what people physically say, and it's the actual meat of what is discussed. Technical content, it turns out, is also what people tend to overanalyze and take too seriously.

Have you ever had a quick message exchange with a person where you got the message completely correct, but the person telling it to you said it completely wrong?

"Hey, which color do you want?"

"Buy me the blue one."

The person then proceeds to buy the red one, much to the content of the person who asked for the blue color.

This situation happens regularly. These examples should clue everyone in that communication between people is so fluid that it goes beyond words. Those who see the value in earning influence from others consistently and strategically will avoid spending nearly any time cleaning up someone's technical content and will focus their attention on listening, asking questions, and guiding conversations.

Instead of letting technical accuracies get in the way of communication, assist the person in making statements that you ought to know.

The flow of technical content can be guided by you.

Everyone needs to make decisions, especially leaders. Decisions are based on a multitude of inputs, especially facts. Facts come from technical content that people provide. Yet, nobody knows what facts you need to make decisions. As a result, you ought to consider helping guide them to the facts you need. If you haven't gotten to the intent yet, steer the person into telling you the intent. Once you have found the intent, steer the person into telling you enough facts for you to gain a picture in order to act on.

> Since leaders often earn influence by
> solving problems through interactions with
> other people, it is imperative that they
> know what problems they *actually* need to
> solve. This is achieved by searching for only
> enough details to get it done quickly.

Repeat back what you have understood

A really effective aspect of active listening is that if you repeat back to the person what you have understood from them, it gives them a great opportunity to confirm you have it correct.

Using the fewest number of sentences, with the plainest language you can deliver, repeat to the person what you have heard and understood.

This will prompt the person to give you a verbal "yes, that is correct." This ought to put to bed any concern that you have understood, correctly, what they are trying to convey.

Doing this action does not mean that the information is true in the real world; it just means that you've understood the situation at least at the level that the speaker does. And that's good for influence, as well as improving your understanding of what is happening.

CHAPTER 14

Empathy

Empathy is the act of correctly reading other people's emotions.

While empathy was briefly touched on in the listening section, it is an important enough skill for earning influence that it is worth digging in here, and one in which many people desperately need help.

Depending on who you ask, you will get a different definition of empathy. Regardless of those definitions, the following is what is meant by the word empathy:

> Empathy is the act of identifying, correctly, what a person is currently experiencing emotionally.

Empathy is **NOT** about having sympathy for the other person, nor sharing a story about how at some point, you have felt the same way. Empathy is also **NOT** the act of validating or rationalizing the emotion by saying whether or not the person *should* feel this way or they should not.

Empathy is *just* knowing what emotion the person is experiencing in that moment.

Understanding emotions is critical towards one-on-one communications because a person's emotions are *rarely* separate from the communications that they have. If you listen carefully to someone's speech, their emotions wrap the language. Oftentimes, the reason they're speaking to you in the first place is because their emotions are so high about a particular bit of information or a situation that they have no control over the need to hand it over to you.

By knowing what emotion the person is experiencing in that moment, you can then take the appropriate actions that will earn influence with great effect or spend influence wisely.

There is a danger in ignoring empathy.

Three Empathy Mistakes

If you do not develop your empathy skills when you communicate with people, you are likely to get stuck doing any of the following **influence draining activities**:

1. Making the discussion about you, either through statements defending yourself or what it means to you.

2. Insulting the other person by showing how easy it is for you (through simplifying and rationalizing the issue down)

3. Having no connection to the person by focusing on all the issues that the person either doesn't see or doesn't value.

Please re-read these three statements.

Meditate for a moment on how many times you may engage in these behaviors when you interact with people. Every one of these actions creates separation between you and the other person, which disconnects your influence with them. At best, your actions will have no effect; at worse, they will cost you influence.

A solution is to identify, correctly, what emotions are currently being experienced and determine what you really ought to be doing that will earn you more influence (you performing an action) or whether this is the right timing for purposeful spending of influence (getting a person to act).

CHAPTER 15

Use Delegation to Earn Influence

Delegation is passing the chance of obtaining success to another person.

While delegation is most notably known as an action that spends influence, it has the ability to earn you influence if done well. In fact, delegating is an effective way to strategically earn influence.

As a general rule, you should constantly be in the process of delegating tasks. Becoming a leader makes one very aware of how many moving parts are needed, especially for excellence. It is extremely tempting to do these tasks yourself, especially since you are the one who is first realizing they need accomplishing.

However, if you are busy doing the tasks, especially those that other people *can* do, then who is at the helm making sure the whole is going in the right direction?

You must learn to delegate.

Three Basic Rules of Delegation

1. **Delegate the right tasks to the right people.** *You will spend a lot of influence getting your most effective person to take your trash out for you.*

2. **If anyone in the organization can do a task 80% as good as you, you should *immediately* delegate it.** *Consider promoting someone to do the task if they can do it 60% as good as you.*

3. **Never do anything for a person that they can do themselves easily.** *Unless you are making a big deal about serving someone, and then only do it once.*

How to Delegate AND Earn Influence

Earning influence by delegating occurs when the person receiving the delegation believes they are receiving an opportunity.

One example is giving a promotion.

Influence Tip: Ceremonies

Get in the habit of creating ceremonies for people, especially beyond the bare minimum. Ceremonies where people are boosted up, and they become the positive focal point of others' attention, raises them up considerably. Promotion ceremonies are an obvious example of a ceremony.

While most people are familiar with the concept of promoting someone, they may not be familiar with peering behind the scenes and realizing that this action is the same as delegating. The only real difference is how the delegation is presented.

When *the leader* makes a big deal about a task being delegated, the importance of the task is raised up. The person receiving the delegation will see the task as being valuable and that they've *earned* the respect and responsibility to own it.

Influence Tip: Bring Others to Meetings

If there is a meeting where additional work is created, **bring someone with you** who is the person who will oversee its completion. The other person will be able to see what's going on and engage with the topic so that when you turn to them, they will know exactly what it is that you are asking of them. Even if you do not have them manage and run the project, you can have them advocate and assist in its fulfillment. **Always bring people with you.**

CHAPTER 16

Strategies for Earning Influence

The strategies laid out in this book come in the form of who you have to become. By "being" a particular type of person, you will benefit from the increased earnings that these sorts of individuals receive. Each of these strategies has a title associated with them. This is not accidental. By taking on and living these titles, it will allow people to pass the influence you have had on them over to others with ease. Regardless of where you are today, I recommend that you choose at least one or more of these titles and live them.

Become an Educator

The most classic form of an influencer is an educator. The Greeks, having existed thousands of years ago, still influence people's actions daily with their books which seek to inform people how to live well.

How Influence is Earned

Educators earn influence because they give away information that is deemed valuable, regardless of the subject that I learned about in school, in some capacity, that information *felt* valuable. The "best" educators are well known to personally engage students and seek to maximize the amount of information gain on an individual-to-individual basis. Effective educators seek to understand how the student learns and then apply the material to them. **The most influential educators make sure to develop one on one relationships with students.**

Earning Influence Strategically

An educator can earn influence strategically through using their access to students to develop long-standing individual relationships. Once these relationships begin to develop, an educator can then influence the student to take on bigger roles in society, including leadership roles. As students begin networking with other students, further influence is earned by the educator when a good word has been shared. It is not uncommon for educators to leave a place of work and bring his or her network of students with them to engage in projects.

The following are a few ways to earn influence further and faster.

Teach Leadership on the Side

At every opportunity, seek to teach leadership and influence students, regardless of your typical teaching topic. If the class is a math class, encourage a student to start tutoring others on the side in order to further improve their math capabilities.

Act as a Mentor

Ask how a student is doing and seek to understand more about what is going through the head of the student. By becoming a mentor, you will provide students a well-needed outlet for the various things happening in their life. Mentors earn an inordinate amount of influence because often they're saddled with the most difficult and pressing problems to an individual. Further information is provided below about how to maximize mentoring.

Become a Manager

Some mistakenly believe that managers are leaders. Managers are not necessarily leaders, but they are managers.

But it is easy to see in the society we occupy today that managers have a great position to become effective leaders. Managers, by their nature, are entangled among people, and this gives them quite the advantage to those who can wield it. They are usually responsible for solving and preventing personnel issues.

The poor leader version of manager relies entirely upon processes, systems, and rules, versus the leader version, which relies upon their connection with other human beings.

How Influence is Earned

Influence is earned by your position as a manager. Every day that you interact with your people directing them to what is needed, and orchestrating production efforts is how a manager earns influence. A manager earns more when they become concerned about the needs of those they serve versus maintaining their position as a spoke in an organization's wheels.

Earning Influence Strategically

Influence should be earned on a daily, weekly, and monthly basis. If you currently have negativity in your management style, *you need to turn it around as quickly as possible*. If you currently believe that you manage for the betterment of the organization, drop that belief, and internalize, you manage for the betterment of the people who make up the organization, particularly those under your concern.

Become knowledgeable of your people's care, concerns, wishes, and dreams. Get to know their life, and ask them how they're handling their issues. Goals for coworkers are important. Discovering, helping set them, and helping them achieve them, and rooting for them as they go is perhaps the fastest way to earn influence.

The next step is building a leadership culture among those whom you manage, even if they are not managers. Daily, weekly, and monthly talk about leadership. Share leadership principles and traits with those around you. The more you inoculate a culture of leadership, the more it will be adopted. Once your culture becomes people-oriented, the capabilities of the organization will begin to soar.

Become a Top Performer

Becoming a top performer is the most commonly thought of a way to earn influence. People believe that if "I'm the best", then people will listen to what I have to say. Just look at movie actors if you want to see the misguided and arrogant belief in action. In reality, influence is not actually earned from your technical talent (you'll see in a moment) but being a top performer can definitely help to put you in an influential seat, perfect for leadership.

In order to be considered a top performer, you must be able to execute on big, complicated, and/or difficult tasks in a much faster way. What can take others days or weeks could take you minutes.

I consider myself a top performer, so let me show you what has to be done to earn influence rather than just patting your own back and being proud of your accomplishments in a vacuum. With the right personality, becoming a top performer is actually **extremely easy.** Read more books, practice more, and volunteer to jump into every difficult problem, then make a life out of doing that.

How Influence is Earned

Influence is earned by demonstrating that you are *consistently* more competent and more reliable than anyone else. As a truly top performer (with a few caveats listed below), you earn access to the ear of decision-makers, and your peers will take what you say more seriously. But this is only half of the story.

In order to actually have influence, **you must have a beaming desire to put those skills to help others,** *always*.

You can see that it is *very* often the case that the most skillful people are the biggest pain to deal with. The increased level of skill often gets to people's heads, and they fail to realize that often their communication skills are poor, they don't listen, and they're difficult to work with.

Skills that are not easily accessible are worthless to others.

So, remember, on one hand, it's a very high level of skill, and on the other, it's the care of and attention to people. Both are required.

Earning Influence Strategically

The top performer earns influence with two groups, somewhat differently. There is management, and then there are peers.

The top performer earns influence with managers by being the "adult in the room." They listen and ask questions to truly understand what's going on. They do not wait to be told what is happening and instead seek to understand, consistently, more than anyone else (even management).

The top performer earns with peers in a different way. While the top performer also listens and asks questions intently to his or her peers, they are looking to see where they may need to look out for the other person. What areas are they troubled with? Often if the top performer is doing a good enough job of creating an inviting environment, they are asked to look over work and comment.

Each time that a top performer's work is focused by a person on a particular problem, and it is done quickly and efficiently, influence is earned. Rarely do people like to struggle, especially when they feel that they appear to others to struggle foolishly on something. A top performer has the ability to earn influence at every step by showing up and seeing if any help is needed.

Remember from the chapter of action that **witnessing a physical thing being accomplished becomes a true belief.**

One of the unique characteristics of being a top performer is you can demonstrate actions that completely blow people away. This leaves them completely open to hearing more or looking for your help on nearly every problem. These people can quickly turn into followers of your leadership if you seek to earn influence.

While the top performer often feels the need to boast, boasting truly is not needed by the top performer. The work itself does plenty of boasting, in usually a non-threatening manner.

Note: If you become a top performer and do not help others with their problems, this performance can begin to work against you. **Remember, people like to know powerful people, so they can use their talents for their own uses.** The top performer earns influence by funneling their performances for the benefit of others.

However, a top performer, who is a leader, knows that they must transfer powers over to others, so they can move forward and take the mantle of leadership, which will require the same zeal for success but in a much broader area of responsibilities.

Be careful of falling in love with your hard-earned
talents at the expense of your purpose.

Become an Advocate

An advocate is a person who champions a cause or a project. Advocates *can* naturally turn into leaders because advocates are already pointed towards a direction they believe is good (also known as a vision). The advocate then needs to build influence and lead people.

How Influence is Earned

Advocates are able to influence because they believe something passionately to the point where it becomes infectious. By caring significantly about something and pouring your soul into it, other people will begin to take notice. The advocate is often asked to share what is so compelling that would make them turn into a champion. Each time the advocate shares what they believe, they have an opportunity to plant a seed that one day may grow into an advocate themselves, especially if cultivated.

The advocate earns influence by providing ideas others had not considered and by casting vision for other people of how they might be able to be a force for good. Advocates give others the hope and belief that they have a purpose. Just by existing and sharing what the advocate knows and believes can be enough to build influence.

How to Earn Influence Strategically

The advocate can earn by weaving leadership ideals into their discussions with others. By encouraging others towards the cause and encourage others to take up the mantle of leadership, the advocate's cause can begin to build momentum. The advocate must see every person as a potential opportunity, valuable in their own right, even if the person does not necessarily immediately adopt their ideas. In fact, the biggest miss-step someone can do trying to convince others to join a cause is to make other people believe even for a moment that they are somehow "the enemy", turning what could be a valuable discussion into building allies.

As with all strategies, valuing people is extremely important. The advocate should reduce their own value in the eyes of others and instead continually and constantly highlight the value that others bring by joining the cause. The more you give to people, the more they'll remember you.

Become a Networker

There are many people who do not believe in networking. But depending on what your ends are, a networker can be a great person to be.

Networkers are people who act as a nexus of knowing people. The value networkers bring for others is that they know other people and what they're "up to in this world". People should be able to rely on a networker to point them to the exact person or group that they're looking for.

How Influence is Earned

Influence is earned in at least two ways as a networker: first by digging for knowledge about people, and second, by helping others find the people they need to know.

When a networker begins the task of understanding who a person is, so they might be able to funnel others towards them, they need to ask many questions. Every question that is asked of others, where the goal is to learn about the person, gives the asker influence.

It shows the other person, by their obvious action, "this person is interested in me." That is one of the easiest ways to earn influence with another person.

The second way of earning influence is by helping others connect. The influential networker not only networks for themselves, but networks for everyone else as well. By making a successful well-made connection between two people, the networker demonstrates their value via *action* and *results.*

How to Earn Influence Strategically

Influence is earned strategically by making the connections between people more valuable and interweaving other networkers into your mix.

One way to improve the value of your connections is by working up the social ladder but still remaining available throughout the ladder. This gives different types of people the ability to reach out and connect with others who otherwise might be extremely difficult to do. This helps facilitate that the higher social ladder gets access to people whom they might have a difficult time finding, while the lower social status person has the ability to rise up, a win for both.

People move through life and pare people and groups out. While you more of the environment you desire, you will be cut off from other people who have the ability to help you out.

The influence and helping power that networkers have is reaching out to gather unknown information (who) and then delivering it to different people who should have it.

Become a Good Person

Have you ever met a 90-year-old lady who never held a job, never held an office, and yet could command any number of people to help them at a moment's notice?

This is the single most valuable title that you can achieve to earn influence. When people associate you as a good person, that tends to mean that you've helped them out and they haven't forgotten it.

When good people ask for assistance, others will come out of the woodwork to help them, even when it's extremely inconvenient.

How Influence is Earned

All influence is earned by doing things for other people. A good person earns influence by being present for others. They listen to their trials and tribulations along with their successes. Good people ask others about how their family is doing, about their hopes and dreams, and what their favorite past times are.

Good people go *way* out of their way to provide for others. Remember that action speaks louder than words, so for the good person to earn, there must be continual and constant action on behalf of others.

How to Earn Influence Strategically

Influence is earned strategically by helping to shape the culture around the good person. By demonstrating and sharing leadership principles and traits, the good person starts to win over others to this way of thinking.

The larger the act of good, the more likely that the action will be told to others. While this is **not** your goal, going way out of your way is what it takes to earn that level of influence over others.

Make no mistake. If you save someone's life or be a shining light when everyone else has given up on someone, those deeds will not go unforgotten.

All of these good deeds act as a built-up currency, that when the time is ready for action to occur, others will move at your command.

Being a good person is worth the investment.

Influence Tip: Do-gooders Need More Risk

For those who are already a "good person", your limit to influence is the level of risk you will take for do-gooding. The typical do-gooder does not move outside their comfort zone very much, and as a result, earns influence continually a little here and there. These do-gooders need to discover going above and beyond. Remember, do-gooders earn influence by doing actions for other people. Sometimes the actions that people really need are not "being nice" but instead not letting a person cheat themselves or needing to physically stand up for them to other people. You are still a good person if you need to knock someone in the nose for the right cause...

For those who are not do-gooders, being able to re-articulate your actions from the context of others is a good way to veil your actions to be good. Those who are not good by nature will struggle to do good activities, making them at best neutral. **This is plenty ok. People take even greater notice of your good deeds because it's clear *you are going out of YOUR way* to help them. And if you are already a high confidence person, you will earn proportionally.**

Notes

Spending Influence

Wisely, Honorably and Purposefully

"Inaction breeds doubt and fear. Action breeds confidence and courage. If you want to conquer fear, do not sit home and think about it. Go out and get busy."

—Dale Carnegie

So here you are. You know what leadership is, you now know you must make a life out of building your character, and you're now going to continually and strategically earn influence with others by taking action. Soon you will have influence overflowing the brim of your cup.

Now it's time to talk about how to get the most out of the earned influence.

> Influence should, as much as possible, be spent
> wisely on an honorable, purposeful end.

It is my duty to show you that this is the case and attempt to compel you to adopt this as your leadership action strategy.

Before we go into depth about the best way to use influence, let's begin with what is meant by spending influence.

CHAPTER 17

Carrying The Load Comes with Costs

Influence is spent every time we ask others to adopt an idea, perform an action, or ask others to carry a burden.

This means that influence is a renewable resource that must be managed and used intentionally if we are to remain a leader.

There is a surprising number of ways that influence can be spent, much of which **people have no idea that they are wearing down their influence with other people.**

You must know that when you interact with people at any given moment, you are either earning or spending influence. Generally speaking, if you are not boosting the spirits of others or helping them in some way, there is a good chance one is spending influence. **Note:** Most people are spending influence.

Below are the 10 most common ways that influence is spent between the interactions of two people:

1. Asking or Commanding someone to do a task.

2. Asking or Commanding someone to listen to you.

3. Overriding someone's preferred approach by using some other approach.

4. Persuading or arguing that someone adopt an idea.

5. Implicitly asking a person to listen to your problems, share your burdens, or to listen to your negative internal emotions.

6. Emotional outbursts in the presence of others, such as frustration or anger.

7. Avoiding responsibility, conducting verbal defenses, or any other excuse attempts.

8. Character flaws, slips of judgment, or callous behavior.

9. Forgetting about something valuable to another person.

10. Time passing without contact.

Note: While many of these can be interpreted as a "negative" or "bad" use of influence, consider withholding judgment about them to see the action in its proper light. As with all actions, whether these are good or bad depends on the context in which they are used. What is universal, however, is that doing these actions draws down a person's balance of influence.

This draw is not always equal.

If you have high influence with a person, and the task for them requires relatively small amounts of influence, then there is an almost negligible loss. The same task with a person whom you have low influence with, done in the same way, can and will create sparks between the two of you.

This is why people who do not intentionally earn influence with others inevitably bounce back and forth with resistance to even minor issues.

Let's look at a married couple or friend scenario for something mundane like taking out the garbage.

The Spender – "Hey, can you
take out the garbage?"

This "ask" in most scenarios is a low influence request. But let's look at potential replies...

"Sure! I'll get it!" – High influence with this person

"Give me a minute." – High-Medium influence

"I don't know. I got it last time. I am not crazy about taking out the garbage. There is this cat out there that is so strange looking, and it stares at me. Can you get it this time?" – Low influence

"Dude. No. Can't you get it? You are always trying to get out of doing any work. I do absolutely everything around here."
– Low to No influence

Notice how the replies increase in size and are less immediate. In order to accomplish the task with the last two relationships, it requires even more "asking" or "persuading" to get the job done. A task, small, with low cost, can require a great deal of effort to accomplish.

While this is a hypothetical scenario, begin to look at your relationships in life and notice if you ask them to do something, how many words are said in reply to your request? When the person begins wavering and begins to add in many words, what they are actually trying to tell you is, **"you do not have enough influence over me to get me to do this. Why not show me how much you value me, and then maybe I'll do it."**

When You Run Out of Influence, You Meet Resistance

People running out of influence with another person is a near- magical phenomenon to see. Poor functioning married couples are some of the easiest to spot. Anytime one asks the other to do something, they either ignore the other person or put up a fight about it. If you hang around them enough, you can see the same request work or blow up spectacularly.

You may be asking, why does the request work sometimes, and other times end in embarrassing drama?

> People constantly straddle the
> line of some influence and no influence.

Highly effective teams of people are willing to do just about anything for each other *regularly*. Low-performing ones are constantly mired in nitpicky topics.

Awareness is important. *Every burden* expends influence.

Those who do not see the burdens they place on others will be unable to why the world resists them.

Have You Ever Blamed Someone Else for Being Stubborn?

Those who do not understand influence well, when they meet resistance, believe "it's the other person". They fail to take 100% responsibility for the job of influencing others. This includes taking 100% responsibility for squandering the influence they have.

Never forget, people are different, they should not be influenced the same, and every time one burdens another, influence is spent.

However, let's make a note. This does not mean that just because we have high influence on someone that we should never expect resistance. In fact, we should expect some resistance, but our ability to get integrated with the resistance is dramatically improved.

Great relationships encourage partners to speak up and make their opinion known, especially in leadership relationships. However, if you have high influence on a person, you are given the privilege to override their preferred approach and go in a different direction. If you are intentionally seeking leadership, people will know that you have their interest and others' interest in mind.

> The difference between relationships with high influence and those with low influence is the degree and character of the resistance to action.

The 10 Ways People Waste Influence

What is sad is how much influence is lost due to lack of self-awareness. People cannot seem to get a good grasp on what they do on a moment-to-moment basis, especially with other people.

In order for you to get off to a strong start, let's take a look at a list of ways that people waste their influence, much like their lunch money. Unlike the previous list of influence spending activities which is a complex discussion, this list is simple. **DON'T DO THESE.**

Take a look at the following list, see where you may or may not be doing these actions, and then consider no longer doing them.

1. Whining or Complaining
2. Talking negatively about people behind their backs.
3. Attacking a person's character directly.
4. Expressing frustration in an "attacking" way.
5. Arguing over or persuading others on the majority of topics, water cooler and trivial alike. (This does not as easily apply to topics relating to your honorable purposeful end.)
6. Overvaluing and aggressively defending something so quickly and easily adopted, such as an opinion.
7. Acting as though objects are more valuable than people.

8. Talking about yourself more than talking about the other person.

9. Side-tracking a discussion by correcting someone's manner of speech.

10. Dredging up old battles and topics long past.

Each one of these actions is pointless unless it is your intent to clash with the person. In the majority of cases, they are expressions of frustration. Frustration is an emotion that comes when you start to feel that you cannot overcome what you are facing, and so you begin to lash out in hopes that it will improve the situation. ***It doesn't.***

In general, nobody cares about someone whining or complaining. Nobody cares about opinions that weren't asked. And absolutely nobody likes to be derailed in a discussion because they said the past tense to a verb instead of the perfect present, ***even the people who do this behavior.***

Earning influence and then using that influence to further big goals necessitates the avoidance of these behaviors. There is little time for petty behavior, improperly steamed frustrations, and talking about "popular topics."

Influence Tip: Earning Influence from Spending

While it is true that carrying the load costs influence, it is possible in some cases to actually earn influence instead of losing it. It depends entirely on the mindset of the person receiving the request. If the person perceives the request as "a gift", then you will earn influence. The key understanding is the word "burden." No burden, no cost.

An example is instead of "asking for more work" from someone, giving them a promotion they have wanted. Another is asking for some artwork to be made by a person who feels they never get to do enough creative work. These aren't burdens.

Leaders who understand the importance of continually earning influence will find ways to reword what they ask for, choose selectively what tasks they ask for and from whom, and will seek ways to elevate the actions others do instead of placing burdens. However, never forget that burdens in life will always be necessary.

CHAPTER 18

Wise Action

Good Experience and Good Judgment

Acting wisely is taking the shortest, most direct path to where you are **really** going.

Getting to where you are really trying to go can be a lot more difficult and requires a lot more consideration than many might think. While many aspects of leadership are difficult enough, the actual act of navigating a team and followers to the end successfully is quite challenging. This is where wise actions come in.

> Wisdom is an absolute necessity
> for achieving victory.

Wisdom Answers the Necessary Questions

How do you know if the actions that are being performed are actually leading you in the right direction?

How do you know if the actions performed are having any effect at all?

How do you know if the actions performed are not actually moving you backward, or are moving you forward but at the cost that you won't reach the end?

Am I asking the right person to do the job?

It is these types of questions that using wisdom seeks to provide the guiding light.

The following are the dimensions of decision making where wisdom plays a role:

1. What actions should be performed?
2. When should the actions be performed?
3. Who should perform the action?
4. Where should the actions be performed?
5. How should the actions be performed, such as, in what sequence?

Even if you know the who, what, where, when, why, and how "in your gut", without verbalizing them, especially to others, it will be difficult to take action on them.

Influence Tip: Compel Others to Answer

Every one of these questions need an answer, but it's *not* necessarily your job to answer all of them personally each time. Compelling followers and "sub" leaders to generate ideas and then present the answers is **exceptionally** effective and highly encouraged. The Marine Corps has built the entire structure of their organization from the idea that decisions like these will be made from the bottom up. Leaders choose the objectives, decide the boundaries for action, and then turn over the implementation details to those beneath them. This happens, again and again, all the way down to the lowest team, the fire team.

Wise Action is The Result of Seeking the Best Available Knowledge

In order to act wisely in these dimensions, leaders must seek the best ideas based on everything they know and everything they have learned. This includes creating a culture where others seek the best ideas as well, not necessarily just their own.

*This is why **leaders** do not care if they share their two cents. They just care about which two cents matters most.*

Listening first and speaking last is extremely important. Using this practice, a leader has the ability to hear what the universe is saying before coming to a conclusion of what to do. While there are absolute limitations to how much you can take in before making decisions (more in-depth later), getting in the practice of listening and seeing what is going on **before** making judgments about what must be going on will pay back with effective choices.

An Author's Perspective

While some know me to be a very talkative person, the majority of the world knows me as a listener. If I meet you, I will find out everything about you. I will look you over briefly and then ask you question after question. I will engage in absolutely any topic that you are interested in going into and even ones that I just want to see how you see them. **By the end of the conversation, I know a lot about you, and you will learn more about yourself.**

However, I reserve all judgments until I see you work.

Once I see a person actually perform actions, then I get a complete understanding of who the person actually is. In a very short amount of time, I have the ability to determine:

> **"Does this person motivate themselves or require motivation?"**
>
> **"Is this person seeking out growth? Are they doing so intensely, or are they passively going through life?"**
>
> **"What is their ability to handle complexity, *now* and in the future?"**

It is completely possible to get **an idea, but not a complete picture** of a situation very quickly just by watching, listening, and then asking a few questions to engage with what others see.

These skills are *required* for developing wisdom about a subject.

You Don't Have All Day. Time Is Of The Essence

If you and your followers are moving forward and followers are performing actions, you no longer have the luxury of taking your time. This is where wisdom needs to meet reality.

At some point in time in your growth, you must release the reins of control. There are simply too many things to know, too many things to do, and too little time to do it all in.

You can see that, in the modern world, heads of companies eventually stop all interactions with customers or vendors. They are instead spending 100% of their time building and focusing on the team's ability to manage vendors and meet and exceed customer expectations.

While there are entire books and fields of study devoted to time management, the point needs to be made that time is a precious resource. There is not unlimited time to figure out "how to do something the *right* way". Improvement comes over time through repetition and iteration.

There is only enough time to figure out how to make *wiser* decisions based on the information you have available.

Influence Tip: Letting Things Fail

You should consider working on your ability to let things fail. It can be extremely difficult to let people fail, especially when you can do something about it, but it is a necessary ingredient for success. We become wise because we have made poor decisions and have done actions where the outcome was not what we expected it to be. This particularly includes actions where the universe, *not just a person*, tells us we've failed.

Effective leaders know that those they influence must reap not just the rewards of their successes but also the results of their failures. One of the easiest ways to start improving your abilities to handle this is by taking a step back and being less engaged with what others are doing, instead, work on your watching skills. So long as nobody gets truly hurt, watch people fail. After all the commotion is over, ask them what they think they could have done differently. In the end, provide a bit of guidance based on what you saw.

Must, Should, and To are Wise Boundaries

A requirement for wise actions is a clear and accurate understanding of the degrees of victory. This is necessary for establishing priorities, at least to yourself, of what needs to happen first. This can then be used to effectively communicate and guide others in efficiently seeking victory.

It is important to understand what needs to be done *now* versus what ought to be done later. Here is a set of words that can be used and reinforced for greater communication of victory conditions.

Musts are actions and conditions that absolutely have to happen because, from an actual technical reality, you cannot achieve the goal unless they are performed.

Shoulds are actions and conditions that *ought* to be performed unless new information contradicts their necessity. Shoulds often are used to reinforce what we value to achieve a greater victory.

Nice-to-Haves are actions and conditions that can bring a greater, nicer victory but are absolutely not required for success. These conditions are generally obtained if it is convenient but ought never to be sought after if it risks the "musts" and "shoulds".

Influence Tip: Limit Your Musts

From my experience, "Musts" ought to be limited to the fewest in number and be used to purely determine the state of *minimum* victory, while "Shoulds" ought to be used to help create a victory that feels substantial. Nice-To-Haves need to be controlled and managed as best as possible because, for many reasons, they sneak up and start to become the primary focuses of the team, to the detriment of the musts.

Depending on the condition's wording, it will change whether or not it's possible that achieving a *should* requires achieving a *must*, the same with *nice-to-haves*. This is usually not the case without careful consideration.

Obtaining all the nice-to-haves, but not every must, then there is no victory. Without conditioning, the problems focused on, the problems that call our attention the strongest are the ones that are focused on. Sometimes they are the toughest problems, and sometimes they are the easiest. Sometimes they are the most fun, or for some reason, people just "believe" they are the most important. Sometimes they are the musts and other times the nice-to-haves. Regardless we have to be vigilant against nice-to-haves taking over focus.

> Wise actions are ones that bring the straightest
> path to what we are trying to achieve.

Getting "musts", "shoulds", and "nice-to-haves" in priority order is essential for making the straightest path.

It is a leader's job to understand what minimum success is with a crystal-clear level of understanding. Then it's the leader's job to influence action that focuses on what is a **must** for victory.

Simple Example for Understanding

Here is an example of a small list of objectives for creating a new school. Take a look and think about how the objectives fit together.

Must

- Find land for building a school.
- Have a dormitory for people to sleep in.
- Have a classroom.
- Have bathrooms.

Should

- Have desks for students to sit at and study.
- Have a cafeteria.
- Have its own flag.

Nice-To-Have

- A flagpole.
- An indoor bathroom.

Looking at this example, it is clear. The nice-to-haves will not achieve the goal of building a school. Instead, they make the final goal of creating a *nicer* school. The shoulds identify a more substantial victory that will ensure things work well. The musts, however, clearly show the necessary conditions for saying one has a school at all. What is a school without being somewhere?

Clarity Prevents Wasted Effort

For a firm reminder, it's necessary to use musts, shoulds, and nice-to-haves, to prevent yourself and others from spending **the majority of your time solving the problems that are not a requirement for success.**

Wasted effort means influence earned is squandered.

If people know their efforts are all a waste, people become demoralized. Influence with them then may come into question. You can now see that it's not just a matter of failing to go in the desired direction, but unwise activity actually spends influence, leaving you with even less influence!

Tasks versus Outcomes – Effective Results

Have you ever asked what a person is doing, and instead of telling you the overall aim of their actions, they tell you the steps they are doing at that moment? Were you confused on why they were doing that task at all? Would you be surprised that they may not know either?

The difference between "tasks" and "outcomes" is significant, and yet most people mistake the two. All wise action requires the focus on outcomes, not tasks. All leaders need to know this difference.

Tasks are the specific actions accomplished.

Outcomes are the desired end results of our actions.

This is a discussion about focus. What is a person focused on? Are tasks their focus, or is the outcome their focus? The reason why it matters is if outcomes are your focus, you will change what tasks you do more readily for one that gets you the outcome with the least resources consumed. When a person becomes task-focused, the task itself becomes the purpose.

The majority of people are task-oriented, and without guidance and focused assistance, they will never accomplish what's needed.

Let's look at two task examples that show where a person's focus is…

Example 1: "I am mailing a letter; in order to do that, you need a stamp, the mailing address, and the return address. Once the letter is all together, you need to walk it out to the mailbox and put the flag up. Then you're all done. Why am I mailing this letter? I was told that mailing a letter might help change legislation that is going through."

Example 2: "I am trying to change legislation, so I am mailing a letter to a representative. If I don't hear anything back in a day, I am going to give them a call or go down to their office. The legislation that they are working on needs to change, even if that means I have to run for office myself."

Can you see the stark difference in these people? Whom do you think is more effective in life? In the first example, they can certainly complete the task well, but if the task doesn't result in anything, they might feel justified that "they've done what they could", whereas the other person will do multiple tasks and continue to act until they've reached the real objective they are shooting for.

> ### Influence Tip: Who is this person?
>
> You can use task and outcome orientation as a means for understanding who a person is that you are meeting for the first time. Task-oriented people are good at repeating a task over and over but are very poor at being able to adjust what they do based on feedback. This can improve with awareness and training.

Those who are task-oriented have a hard time seeing the big picture. It is the details that draw the person in, and their focus will move every deeper into more details. While sometimes the details matter, often deeper details do not matter; they only distract.

Task-oriented people have little ability to determine if a task needs to be performed at all, whereas outcome-oriented people will quickly dismiss the *need* to do something that really isn't a need at all.

> Leaders need to stay focused on vision, resources, and people in order to spend influence well. Outcomes must be what a leader is seeking, rather than tasks.

When Actions Have No Wisdom

By this point, you should have a very strong understanding of what the word "wise" means as it relates to spending influence and guiding others in their efforts. Before moving on, let's take a last look at what happens when actions have no wisdom.

The world is awash in wisdomless actions.

While there is no doubt the world has operated wisdomless in the past, today is particularly troubling given the size, scale, and scope of wisdomless behavior. In the United States circa 2020, the population has become so completely crooked in its concerns that nearly all aspects of life have been boiled down to making money and consuming goods and services. And while the statistics overwhelmingly show that there have never been fewer crimes and all signs point to heaven on earth, people feel hollow, worn out, and desire to enact and reenact adversarial politics of the 20th and 19th centuries.

Wisdomless Decisions Lack Holistic Thinking

Wise actions take into consideration as many important aspects as possible, such as people, cultures, and the future. Wisdomless actions focus on single results, often to the detriment of everything else.

People orient their lives around making money and solving problems for businesses, yet never ask whether they should assist a business that is manipulating its customers.

People purchase a product to solve a problem, yet the cause of the problem is never addressed, and the problem doesn't go away. Now they're poorer, have more stuff, and still haven't addressed the problem.

Non-holistic thinking is pervasive without wise action.

Wisdomless Actions Squander Resources

There is a reason why the saying for assume is "if you assume, you make an ass out of u and me." People who assume get themselves and others into trouble. Assumers compel people into action based on faulty and unvetted information, causing others to focus in the wrong direction and work on the wrong activities.

Assuming is an unwise activity, and with all unwise activities, it wastes influence that has been hard-earned.

> Assumptions are the product of a lazy approach to life. These attitudes are ultimately toxic to influence, if not immediately, with followers knowing that a leader is speaking beyond their knowledge then later when the results make themselves apparent.

Influence Tip: What do you know?

The clearest way to stay away from assumptions is to get crystal clear with what you actually know. Ask the question, "Do I know this to be true?" If you can say that with very reasonable confidence, then that's a good start. Avoid lazy thinking and lazy statements.

Lack of Wisdom Leads to Going Too Far

If you are lacking in wisdom, you will not know when to stop going in a particular direction. Like a train that has hopped its rails, actions lacking in wisdom continue to go down paths that don't matter.

This is a much more difficult matter to understand than it might first appear. Especially if you are the one who goes too far, your habits, your approaches, your patience (or lack of) for people all could be questionable.

Do you wait around for people who have low effectiveness longer than you should? Consider focusing your attention on the people whom you know are highly effective.

If you don't know when to stop, or others don't know when to stop, efforts will be wasted going in the wrong direction. Maybe at first, it was the right direction, but eventually it turns into the wrong direction.

> Unwise actions can help you win battles with short-term victories, but eventually, the results of lack of wisdom reveal themselves as you lose the war.

Practical Tips on Wise Actions

> Wisdom is earned through intention,
> experience, and reflection.

While wisdom is earned continually over time in one area, it can also be earned in different areas and accumulate together. This means that there are areas that, if you improve in, it will help you improve in other areas as well. The question then becomes, "how does one go about earning wisdom?"

> Think → Do → Reflect

Start Thinking Strategically.

Strategic actions are the hallmark of someone who is using wisdom. Remember, a strategy is a series of planned actions that are designed to achieve large goals. In order to execute a strategy, the following elements are absolutely required.

1. More than 1 action is chosen.

2. Actions are conducted before, during, and after other actions in a sequence.

3. There is a singular intended result as part of a larger goal.

How much of your day do you spend doing one action to achieve one outcome?

Are your actions sequenced, planned, and timed to achieve as great of an effect as possible?

How many of your actions have no purpose at all?

Are your actions coerced? Are these actions always in response to others rather than in the direction you intend?

> Building strategies will give you the ability to think
> clearly and plan for how you, and others, will be
> able to do what needs to be done.

Get Separation from "the Tribe" to Earn Wisdom

Wisdom is the product of reflection after actions. In order to get that reflection, after interacting with others, you need space to think.

If you want to be able to see the bigger picture and act in a larger capacity, you cannot do it when you are swamped with the "problems of the day", especially if they are solving the *daily* problems of others.

For some, separating can be hard to do but know that it's necessary for gaining wisdom.

Nearly every person has a hard time ensuring intentional separation happens.

- Do-ers want to keep working.
- "People persons" want to keep connecting.
- Even isolated or strategic thinking types want to squander their lone time with unproductive thinking or tasks smaller than what they ought to be considering.

The "Do-er" types need to be able to *do* tasks at a much higher level. The do-er is doing the small actions instead of the bigger ones. The do-er fails to automate, delegate or drop tasks, instead deciding that they "must be done" *NOW*.

What the "people person" is missing is their habitual hanging around others, which makes it nearly impossible for them to adopt a genuine opinion about anything or even a true mosaic of what is out there. Instead, this person, a social butterfly, floats from one person to the next adopting the ideas, beliefs, and feelings from one person and changing them with the next person they meet. Stepping back might make them realize they ought not to spend so much time listening to certain people and instead focus on listening to others for particular reasons. By doing so, they may remain *more consistent* and build a reputation that crosses from person to person.

The isolated person is missing that much of their work is "their size and lower." They do not work on projects that challenge them or push them outside of their comfort zone. Without getting away and taking a hard look at what they are doing, they, like the doer, fail to see that they could be working on more important issues.

Separation creates space.
Space creates an opening for a bigger perspective
to exist. Leaders need perspective for wise action.

Learn how to Manage Money

Learning the basics of managing money is a great way to learn to be wise. Are you able to set a budget and stick to it? If you can set a budget but fail to stick to it, why?

Managing money may seem like a strange topic for this book, and even earning wisdom, but it's more about the exercise of working with money, setting limits, and building intentionality with what you do with it.

Is your money squandered on expenses when it ought to be going towards the acquisition of new assets?

Are you guaranteeing you are increasing your savings every money by moving a percent of your income to the side, **first** before even paying your housing or living expenses?

There are too many books and topics on managing money to go over here, but it's worth stating that managing your own personal finances well is part of the road to acting wisely.

Begin Reflecting on The Results of Your Actions

The final act in building wisdom is reflecting as accurately and clearly as you can on the results of your actions.

Reflection raises your awareness

Awareness is the ability to see more; more aspects, more angles, more intentions by people, a bit more of everything. Your awareness of yourself, how you talk, dress, behave, and even your beliefs have dramatic impacts on what happens to you in your life. And yet most people don't spend the time to see the things.

Without reflecting on our actions, we fail to get the larger connections in life and see how many things are connected together.

A poor life view of others makes you irritable to deal with, often requiring others to dance around you. This, in turn, continues to feed your beliefs about them as your observed experience shows that your poor life view of others is true. **Reflecting on what you believe will give you the ability to shape and change what you believe, which in turn will shape the world around you differently.**

Like all skills, reflection takes practice, practice, practice.

It takes considerable time to develop your ability to reflect. Reflections will display judgments. There will be judgments about yourself, about your assumptions about "what could have been", and about other people. Of which, many judgments will be incorrect, unhelpful, and focused on the wrong things.

Remember, one can only gain strength at a skill by setting the intention, doing it, and then thinking about it. This includes even the act of "thinking about it."

Influence Tip: Starting Intentional Reflection

An effective way to do intentional reflection is to set up a list of reflective questions and go back to them regularly (weekly). *"Did your actions have intention?"* If not, start doing things intentionally.

"Did the results match what your intentions were? If not, why not?"

"How can you change what you're doing to meet your intentions?"

These are the sort of questions that I would recommend asking to improve your wisdom.

CHAPTER 19

Purposeful Action

A reason for existence

Why should anyone follow you? Is it because of the way you talk to them? Is it because you help them with small problems? Or is it just because of a subconscious attraction to your disposition?

There are endless ways to describe your influence over others, yet if we look at the question words for understanding, we'll find one that stands out the most.

"What" tells a person exactly what you're doing now or intend to do.

"Where" tells a person the location you are going.

"Whom" tells a person who all is involved.

"How" tells a person the method for achievement.

"When" tells a person the time that events should happen.

"Why" tells a person the driving force behind everything you do.

Most of these words have little influential value. However, **"why"**, on the other hand, is different.

"Why" is the *real reason* people follow you.

Purpose is distilling "Who You Are" and "What You Value"

Purpose is so critical to leadership. Since people are influenced by others for the sake of improving the position of themselves, your *why* becomes the trust between you and them. Purpose says what you value and is the bases of how they will be improved.

If you value "family" and that's part of your purpose, then those who believe in "family" too will be willing to listen to you, on the off chance that their family may benefit as well.

A leader isn't *just* an influential "man or woman"; they are the leader of a *direction* and *end*, a purpose.

For some, naming their values is easy and natural, and for others, it requires introspection and triangulation. But once you've found your values, you can begin to discover your purpose.

Purpose is Found Through Discovery

The purpose of one's life cannot be found through sitting and pondering. This leads to a wandering mind disconnected from what's real. The longer one sits, the more likely to come to the conclusion that *"there is no purpose at all."*

Personal purpose *exists.*

While one could question if one is born with a purpose, this philosophical conundrum is unnecessary to answer. Purpose is accepted. Purpose is found. Purpose is discovered.

Purpose is found by **doing and experiencing,** not through reading about someone else's life.

Warning: Books are not *your* experience.

While books and reading can expand awareness and are great for ideas, be on guard to the belief that they will give you purpose. There is much folly in the consumption of too much information to the detriment of actual tangible experience. Consumption of information delays action and often points one into areas that are outside of one's true value system.

It is only through action and personal experience that real purpose can be discovered.

Finding purpose is not complicated. Get out there into the real world, look around, see what is going on, and make determinations based on what you *know*.

Once You've Found Purpose, Communicate It

If you have found solid ground on purpose, purpose must be the center point of your communications. Begin communicating this purpose with everyone.

For those who have not done this before, communicating *your* purpose can feel daunting. You must stand firm when you state *your* purpose. Instead of saying "someone ought to do something about it" or other passive phrases, say to the world, "I am going to do something about it".

YOU must be the person who takes the mantle, marshals the resources, and see the purpose through to fulfillment.

It is the brazen discussion of purpose in front of others that influences them. This discussion builds their confidence and builds their strength to believe it is possible. In almost everything you do, your purpose needs to be the driving force.

Purpose is the rallying call that snaps people to attention and focuses them towards what you are driven towards. Those who are standing on the sidelines quietly have the chance to make themselves available to you *only* if they know the purpose.

If your purpose is not strong enough, if it is not grounded in a reality that others can get behind, forward progress will be elusive and sporadic.

> Only a conscious effort to drive purpose and seek those who desire its fulfillment will lift the sails of accomplishment.

But this communication is for you too

Never forget influencing ourselves is never-ending; we must communicate purpose to ourselves.

If you have chosen a purpose larger than yourself (a requirement for leading others), then you will need to sustain yourself over the long term. Communicating your purpose to yourself continually strengthens your desire to see its fulfillment, pulling you through thick and thin, dull and exciting. There is no success without purpose.

Help Others to Own the Purpose and Drive It for You

Remember, leadership is about getting others to do actions. At every single layer of leadership, a leader ought to get others to do those actions. *Going further, a leader ought to get others to do those actions.*

Purpose is no different. Help others discover their place and purpose, and help them communicate it to others as well.

As other people begin to drive purpose, you can continually take a step back to watch and gain a fuller picture of what is going on. While you must always carry the mantle of the purpose of your leadership, do not fear yielding over the development of this purpose to those whom you directly lead.

Helping others develop purpose is a process that takes time, requires nurturing and a bit of mentoring.

But the results are worth it.

Watching other people adopt purpose and communicate it to others is a phenomenon that has to be experienced to appreciate.

Leadership without Purpose *is* Manipulation

If you compel a person to perform an action where the person does not know the purpose, you are drifting into costly manipulation.

Every compelled action has a cost, but depending on how the action is framed and the mental state of the person, the cost can be dramatically different. Sending a person into action without knowing why they are doing the action has the highest cost and lowest return.

This is why purpose is so fundamental.

From the very beginning of doing the action and throughout the whole activity, the person wonders, "why am I doing this?", "why is this so important?" Instead of focusing on accomplishing objectives and being present to change at a moment's notice, their attention is focused on a negative concern.

People flounder in life if they do not know why they are doing what they are doing.

The mind begins searching for a purpose, **any purpose**. What was originally a follower and a helpful person may turn against you. Depending on the way the wind blows, the person may fill themselves with anxiety, lack of hope, and embarrassment. All of which will be pointed at you.

Without a purpose, people will blame you for absolutely everything.

Simple problems that would normally be handled without problems become show stoppers. People will call back for assistance and for additional motivation constantly. Every action performed will be at less than full strength. The person will not take ownership of any of their actions.

All of this because they do not know the purpose of their actions. This situation is completely avoidable, but only if they have a strong solid purpose that they can get behind.

Leadership without purpose requires YOU to constantly manipulate in order to move progress forward.

If you are spending your time manipulating, when will you have time to lead?

Practical Tips on Finding a Compelling Purpose

For some people finding a truly compelling purpose seems like a hard if not impossible task. You might ask, "how will I know when I have found it? Will there be an ah-hah moment?" Here are some practical tips on finding a purpose that is compelling enough for you to take up the challenge of leadership.

Start by Living in the Real World

While it was explained earlier that purpose is discovered by getting out in "the real world," it seems clear that in the year 2020, even figuring out what the real world is can be confusing. There is an unbelievable amount of human and "systems" messaging that tries desperately to grab your attention. But yet, a compelling purpose that matters only exists outside of convoluted higher-order concepts that humans invent.

Spend Time in Nature

If you sit long enough, observe the outdoors and interact with it, you will find the real world.

The great forces of the cosmos do not acknowledge the concepts coined by humans, nor their concerns about them.

What this means is if you are looking for a purpose grounded in reality, you can begin to look at nature for signs and clues of where to focus. Regardless of what the "techno-fantasy" novels and speakers of today say, **the universe is real.**

It may be tempting to believe that there is no meaning in the universe and that it is all chaos and disorder, but through careful observation, you can see the reverse is true. The patterns of nature provide focusing clues.

Here are but a few themes you may find:

- Life desires to exist.
- Life grows on top of death.
- Life works together in a complex harmony.

All *life* exists within specific contexts that contain specific
large and tiny life that can only live with a specific
combination of water, mineral, and energy cycles.

Observing and interacting with nature shows what is *truly true*, irrespective of one's desire to look at it or think about it.

By spending time in nature, you detoxify your thinking

If you spend a significant amount of time in an office, at institutions,
on the internet, or other locations where great numbers of humans
congregate, you will become more and more mixed up in ideas that
are questionably real.

When you spend time quietly immersed in nature, you will improve
your ability to see what matters. **There is a reason why people leave
"the busy life" and move out into the country for "the quiet life."**

People inherently know that more time outdoors and less time
around cities is good for your health. It is also good for setting priorities in one's life.

Spend Time Around Children

There used to be a television show entitled "Kids say the darnedest
things." This television show attempted to portray children as either
a sage of wisdom or completely crazy based on what they would say.
Here is what is true.

If you want to know people at a fundamental level, interact with
young children. They embody the core attributes of being human;
their little hands carry no baggage, and if you are attentive enough,
you will start to see how people *ought to interact.*

Children can remind you of the basics of interacting with others.

Working with children will not show the greatest ambitions people can have, but it will show you what ambition looks like.

Working with children will not show the greatest evils people can have, but it will show you how people become discouraged, frustrated, and angry.

Working with children will not show the power of mobs, but it will show you that people love to "follow the leader" when it's compelling.

Spending time around children is living in the real world.

Children are often just trying to have a good time and use the basic building blocks they have. When you are around them, you will not be far from reality, even if they are just playing pretend.

Spend Time Around Death

While spending time around children will help you with the earliest of life, spending time around those who are on death's door or have already passed will show you more of what the real world actually entails. Death is likely not what you think it is.

Those who have gone through near-death experiences often feel happier, more elated, and have a higher thirst for life.

Why?

Because they have a new "lease on life." Life feels more vibrant, more brilliant, and they realize how valuable life is, regardless of one's conditions.

Death can be found absolutely everywhere in nature.

Tree branches that have gone brown, grass from the past season now turned browned, mulching the ground, and young sapling trees that never made it into mighty oaks. Each and every one of these provides the fodder for the next growth.

As the seasons pulse life and death, the next stage of life grows on yesterday's death. Observe this with your own eyes and mind. Seeing and understanding the inner-workings of nature provides perspective on life as a whole.

These real-life observations have the ability to spark your purpose.

Your mind is looking for purpose even now. It requires the right inputs to develop the purpose that you are truly looking for.

It is only the proper real-life simulation that provides the purpose that you are searching for. Whether it is the origins of life and death or observing nature in its rawest form, your purpose is found *out there*.

CHAPTER 20

Honorable Action

Of High Respect

The final word for spending influence well is honorable. This word is far more complex than the others and, when taken out of context, is dangerous for victory. But when instituted properly, it will keep a leader and the leader's followers driving forward, making the progress they *ought* to make.

> Honorable actions are actions that express a
> person's highest values.

The overall purpose of your leadership and the actions that you influence people to do **should be honorable.**

The reason you have leadership and influence at all is because the person believes yielding themselves over to you will make them better off.

This civil teamwork requires that for you to keep influence with them, you avoid compelling actions that contradict them and instead funnel them towards the actions they **ought to do but might not do on their own.**

As a word of moral caution, if you focus their efforts on other-than-honorable purposes, you are engaging in either deception, fraud, and/or manipulation.

This isn't to say that people will be excited to perform all compelled actions, just that by doing the actions, it should be an expression of their personal highest values. Meeting one's own values can be difficult, even honorable ones.

This is why leaders exist. This is why you exist.

Leaders exist to push, pull, cajole, or otherwise get people to do the actions that **they know they *ought* to perform.** The leader's vantage point helps them see what others are missing and helps navigate a world of unimaginable complexity.

In the face of daunting odds, difficult times, or even basic self-growth, fear and self-preservation rise above our highest values. These are the times that test a leader's ability to earn great influence quickly and their ability to expend influence for good reasons.

Honorable is About How Something Gets Done

Honorable isn't about doing what one does effectively; that's wisdom. Honorable isn't a reason for itself; that's purpose. Honorable is about taking people on the path in a way that they *should*.

Because you see the word "ought" and "should", you should continually remind yourself; these are words of **values**. Actions as expressions of higher values *are* honorable actions.

Figuring out what one "ought to do" and one "should do", can be difficult if you are out of touch with making decisions based on values. Everyone earns their own personal awareness and to act honorable, must begin to become aware and gravitate to what one truly values. Failing to become aware of one's highest values leads to sleepwalking, where one's daily "shoulds" and "ought tos" lead to self-ruin.

Honorable Actions Empower, Dishonorable Actions Disempower

When people do actions that they do not find to be honorable, their self-worth is lowered by completing them. This is the life of regret and embarrassment.

When people do actions that they feel are honorable, it elevates them to a higher level. Their confidence increases, and they *earn* further belief that what they are trying to obtain is possible.

Honorable requests keep people disciplined and focused, while dishonorable requests cause people to become cynical.

Honorable actions build momentum, while dishonorable actions lead to quagmires.

Words of honorable actions spread and garner influence, while words of dishonorable actions create animosity and decay.

While everyone is not motivated by talk of honor, ***nobody wants*** to live in an environment where dishonorable actions are occurring, nor do they want to engage in dishonorable acts themselves.

Without honor, toxic natures pop out. The seven deadly sins creep into the behavior of people. Toxic gossip begins. And worst of all, mutiny, plotting, and scheming naturally forms to topple the leader who is sleepwalking to disaster.

Instead, honorable acts can become the catalyst that moves purpose forward.

Honorable actions extend the power of influence. Honorable actions begin to insulate people against toxic outside cultures and destructive distractions that are begging for their attention. Honorable actions build an **inside** culture.

Seek not to motivate others purely with abstract
talk of values and honor, instead motivate them
by showing them how to do what they know
they ought to be doing.

Are there downsides to this honorable Mandate? Yes.

The word honorable is an ideal. As with all ideals, idealistic and out of control, people take an ideal to the extreme. A pragmatic observation shows that people can become too attached to maintaining the looks of an ideal over getting done what needs to get done.

Without wisdom, honorable activity on its own can lead down the long path to the end or prevent the team from reaching the endpoint entirely.

In the end, honorable intent exists to challenge people to push forward when the people don't want to, give a motivational boost to those doing adult actions when they just want to be children, and ensure we're meeting our mandates as leaders to better those who come into contact with us as best as we can.

You will never lose sight of getting what you
envision, so long as you act honorably, earn
wisdom, and stay focused on purpose.

CHAPTER 21

Practical Tips on Spending Influence Well

The following section details practical tips on spending influence. While all of these are not necessary, if some of these ideas appeal to you, then adopt them. If some of these tips spark other ideas for you to improve your spending habits, then take those. Regardless, improving your earning and spending is a worthwhile investment throughout your life.

Learn and Practice the Basics

Spending influence requires asking for action. While much of our influence can be spent implicitly asking for action, we ought to ask for it concisely and clearly.

Practicing Tasking People

Tasking people involves directly or indirectly "asking" a person to do an action. It involves getting a person to put a task on their plate.

"Will you take care of this phone call?"

"Are you able to run by the store?"

For some people, tasking comes naturally. And for those people, consider skimming this section.

For everyone else who is not sure if they have "natural" leadership skills, consider trying to task people at the very basic level.

Begin to get the idea in your mind that you **can** get other people to do what you want them to do, simply by asking for it. Once you've acknowledged this is possible, **just ask.**

While one can be concerned about not making mistakes, the best way to figure out that you need to improve your spending of influence is to get the results that come from spending it unwisely, for less than honorable reasons, and for no real purpose.

Ask for a person to do something that gets them in trouble. Ask for a person to do something slightly silly or self-deprecating. And ask a person to do a series of tasks that have no purpose at all.

Watch the result of these tasks, **but note that you can still get these tasks executed.**

See what it looks like when a person doesn't know why they are doing a task and how poorly they perform it. Watch you lose extra influence when a person feels they have been led unwisely. Take into consideration how much influence is consumed when you get a person to jump up and down, touching their nose and patting their belly, *and then ask them to do it a second time.*

Yet these sorts of tasks are asked for every day. **You can ask for a task too.**

If you have a spouse, **task your spouse.**

If you are living with your parents, **task your parents.**

> While tasking others does not make one a leader, a leader compels others to do actions. In order to become a leader, you must become skillful in compelling others to do actions, including making the mistake of asking for less than honorable actions, tasks better not performed at all, and tasks that lack any real purpose.

Learn to Give Commands

Commanding a person is the act of concisely telling a person to do a specific action. Commands are not "requests"; they are not "asks"; they are direct statements for another person to act upon. Commands, *if performed well*, require few words, require no interpretation, and cause **no hateful feelings** by the recipient.

Commanding is a rarely utilized skill yet commanding when exercised properly is so powerful that it is worthy of practice and obtainment.

When prefaced with a quick description of "why" someone is about to do a number of actions (purpose), commanding is a very effective way of spending influence well.

Many mistake commanding as a desperate attempt to force someone to do an action. This isn't commanding; this is a desperate attempt to force someone to do an action.

Commanding, when performed with excellence, *sounds neutral in tone* and is non-threatening. Direct statements without any coloring, such as "pick up that trash", in a way, cause a "click" in a person's mind to feel as though that action is important enough for them to perform it. As a result, the person complies. While there is no real reason to know why this works so well, the best explanation is confidence.

People like to follow others who have confidence, and only confident and powerful people command

Commands only come from people who are confident that the commands will work. Like a wizard performing a spell, those who **"attempt it"**, have mixed results, but those who *do it* succeed.

Never forget that those who follow us, who follow after us. So long as we are acting wisely, with honor, and with purpose, others who begin to command are doing what they believe they should. When you begin giving commands, other people who are confident will start giving commands as well. **This is a good sign, especially if they are doing so well.** If you find yourself naturally resisting their commands and/or getting frustrated, you may need to take stock of what is happening. Are they commanding in such a way that causes you to take offense? **Consider whether or not you command in such a way that others take offense.**

Get Others to Command Themselves

A slightly less direct way of expending influence than giving commands directly is getting others to command themselves. This can be done in the form of "asking for action."

Asking for action is a powerful way to both compel action but also build buy-in.

What you do is ask a question, where they feel compelled to say "yes".

Instead of telling someone to do something (**known as commanding, which is highly recommended**), asking a question is a much softer approach that builds buy-in. The issue with commanding is that it sets up a situation where a person feels like they must become an adversary not to do the action, whereas this approach opens up a window for them to politely try not to, and giving you the option to renegotiate with them.

"Will you do this?"

If you build up a dialogue with a person with the intent of getting them to do something, they may uncover a desire to convince themselves to do it. If you ask them if they **"will"** do something, it puts the person in a position where their natural desires to be cooperative will get them to say **"yes."** While this approach works on the majority of people who are cooperative types, this may work from time to time with people who are not so cooperative.

"Can you do this?"

This question taps on a person's ability to show off. If you ask a person if they **"can"** do something, it puts the person in a position where their natural desire to appear strong and to overcome will corner them to say **"yes."** When asked well, the person does not see the ask as a burden, but rather a self-call to prove themselves. This approach is highly effective with people of all different types, but especially with people who are "challenge oriented" or like to be in control of their life.

Move Faster

This suggestion may seem like an odd one to some, but moving faster in life, in general, is an effective way to get people to do actions that you ask them. When people walk quickly (also known as moving with a sense of purpose), others tend to believe they are *really* trying to get somewhere. This somewhere must be for a good reason to cause the person to move quickly.

The body language of "moving with a sense of purpose" causes others to feel slightly uneasy. People can sense the chaos that must be causing the other person to move quickly. As a result, they are much more likely to listen if you engage with them; after all, listening to you might prevent chaos from falling into their lap as well.

Moving faster works for commands, requests, and general "asking for help."

Keep Track of Influence in and Out

If you are an organized type of person, the following section outlines a method for tracking influence earned and spent in a physical format.

Create a relationship binder that holds the intentional efforts you have had for earning influence and the tasks you have asked them to accomplish.

Get a 3-ring binder and fill it with paper. On each page, create a mini bio on all of the people that you know that you are interested in truly influencing. This would likely include family members, friends, peers, work bosses, managers, employees, community members, etc. Literally, anyone that you wish to influence or lead.

Every time that you intentionally interact with the person, keep notes on the interaction. Try to focus on understanding how your chosen actions impacted the other person.

How well did you perform? What was your delivery, and how did the person interpret what you said? Did they adopt your request, or did they require considerable coaxing?

If you keep track of these events in order, you have a chance of understanding the patterns of your communications with this person and better influence how you approach them in the future.

Take Workshops and Courses on Communication

Learning how to communicate is an important investment, especially for those who have not worked extensively in the area of effective communications.

For those who wish to spend their hard-earned influence wisely, effective communication is a must to learn. However, communications cannot be learned in a vacuum.

It just so happens that there are communication workshops that you can attend to experience those who are effective communicators and work on your communication skills.

Toastmasters is one of the most commonly available ways to learn about speaking.

Toastmasters helps people cultivate their ability to speak publicly, open and freely. The workshops can be challenging as they put the person in uncomfortable positions to speak about topics that they may know little about. All of their efforts assist the person in being able to speak freely, but also with clarity for a listener to understand.

Hire Another Person for Small Labor

There is nothing like hiring a person and paying them from your own pocket that will teach you to be concise with your communications and thinking. While a person waits on you to figure out what you need them to do, they are earning money while you spend yours.

Remember, spending influence is much like spending money. You can only spend what you have, and you have to spend smartly if you want to get something done.

If you hire a person, you immediately become "the leader." The person coming to you for work is looking for what they need to do to get what they want. This puts you in a position of power to exert influence. In most small labor situations, this comes in the form of commanding and direct. Hiring a person gives you some feel of leadership, even if the leadership only exists, not because you have earned it from them, but because you have earned money.

Why Are You Hiring Them? – Purpose

Hiring people to do jobs, even if they are small jobs, will get you in touch with the need to clearly understand what objectives you are trying to reach and conveying these objectives in as few words as possible. The more words you give them, the more frustrated the other person is likely to become. Consider for a moment that for small labor jobs, the person being hired is there to do the work, not chat with you.

But if you do not say enough, the person may feel uncertain about what exactly it is they are there to do. They are there to do **the work.** So, what is *the work,* exactly? If you put yourself in their position for a moment, think about the following statement:

There is nothing more confusing than being hired for a job and nobody telling you what to do or seemingly care whether you work.

This may seem like an odd statement. "Who wouldn't want to be paid but not have to do anything for it?"

While some people really *like the idea* of being paid to do nothing, it turns out that people actually yearn to feel some reason for existence. Even doing the same repetitive activities for days and weeks will induce this same effect. When you hire labor, especially over days' time, and you don't give them ample reasons to be there, they will stop showing up.

Let me make this clear.

People will leave your side, *even if you try to pay them* if you don't figure out the right level of interaction they need.

Leading people, regardless if you pay them or not, requires the exact same foresight. It is imperative that people know why they are there, and they, **themselves,** must develop a clear understanding of how they personally can contribute. If a person cannot understand how they can contribute to whatever may be going on, this is a clear failure of leadership. Yet, it happens every day, even in "leadership" based organizations.

Hire Wisely to Get the Job Done – Wisdom

The hiring experience will also teach you the value of people. Not all people are valuable for the same tasks, and some seem to not know they are terrible at something, such as organization.

Some people require a considerable amount of hand-holding, while others can get the gist of what you are looking for instantly and will get busy getting it done faster and better than you could.

The most powerful leaders lead teams where nearly every decision and implementation are handled by the team and not the leader.

In order for this to be possible, you must have a clear purpose and have self-motivated people who are clear about the value that they bring to the table.

While commanding and directing is a way to do direct communication, it should be used with some intelligence. **Telling people what to do is very, *very* costly.** Not only does it cost you in influence spent, but it also costs you in your own time to focus on the problems of others.

All the more reason to make sure that you are wise with your time and projects.

Honorable Labor

Yes, hiring people to work on a project of your choosing is an opportunity to work on your re-enforcing the honorableness of other people. As a reminder:

> Honorable actions are actions
> that express a person's highest values.

Those who often have the need and means to hire for assistance often don't because they believe that the work they'd be hiring for is beneath the work of others. Often these people are too embarrassed to have someone else clean up their mess.

And yet, this belief about being beneath the work of others couldn't be further from the truth.

Work for people is often an expression of who they are and their current frame of reference. If people are responding to your ads or willing to commit to at least trying to work, this is a sign that they value performing tasks for pay.

Showing up as Labor is a sign of responsibility.

If you hire a person, consider that this is an opportunity to work on your ability to reinforce and acknowledge the values that people possess. Showing up to do a hard labor task is often a sign that they have some respect for responsibility. **Feel empowered to let them know that you respect the work that they are doing.**

This is quite an opportunity, if you see to it, to embolden a person's spirits by letting them know that you highly value the work that they do and what it means to you and others. By having a great appreciation for the work they are doing, it raises the honor factor of the work considerably.

Now the job isn't just a job; it's something that impacts the life of another person, who happens to be very appreciative.

While all of these actions do build your character and can even earn you influence, this is about building your ability to spend influence wisely, honorably, and with purpose.

> Influence that is spent wisely, honorably, and
> with a purpose is key to achieving something
> greater than yourself.

Become an Effective Leader

Understand How People Work

> *"Management is doing things right; leadership is doing the right things."*
>
> —Peter Drucker, Essential Drucker

Becoming effective at leading and influencing people requires that you understand how people work. This includes understanding how you are influenced every day. Since *knowing* takes experience and time, understanding is the first start. By understanding exactly what is in front of you, you can grow where this book (or others) does not provide the answers.

Those who understand how others work are bolstered against untrue beliefs, cynicism, and a lifetime of needless frustrations; All are conditions of looking at the world with disgust rather than understanding.

We can either judge the world to the destruction of ourselves, or we can **lean into these facts and figure out how to use them to the ends we desire.**

CHAPTER 22

Treat Everyone Differently

People are not the same, and leaders must become not only aware but comfortable with this fact. The differences between people are much more profound than "I like pizza" or "I like hamburgers."

People operate in the world so differently that it affects their survival strategies, whether they focus on the past, future or now, how they speak with others, and even what value they see of tools and others. As a result, leaders must quickly understand who is in front of them and choose an appropriate influence approach.

The two most dominating differences in people are.

1. Does the person communicate concretely or abstractly?

2. Does the person focus on cooperation or utility?

Some people *only* speak in concrete terminology. They talk about specific people that did something, somewhere. These concrete types want to hear stories with a beginning, middle, and end with no jumping around.

"I saw John at the library yesterday around 2 pm. Sally met him there, and then they went to the movies. She had this large purple dress on; I kept thinking, 'that's a crazy dress."

Others speak entirely in the abstract. Everything said is a grouping of generalities and concepts. These people rarely point to specific instances where something concretely happened, instead referring to either an abstract model or generalized pattern. This occurs commonly through the use of similes, metaphors, and "sayings."

"You know what's kind of crazy? They have these dress-like things out there that people are buying. They remind me of a pumpkin. I've noticed the only people buying them are middle-aged people who are locked into some other era. Kind of like people who wear bell-bottom pants. This lady Mary I know has one."

Without a conscious effort to change what is said, when concrete and abstract people meet, confusion begins.

When an abstract person speaks, a concrete person does not know why they are supposed to care. When a concrete person speaks, the abstract person becomes frustrated waiting for a concrete person's story to "get to the point".

Influence Tip: Is this person concrete or abstract?

You can determine if a person is speaking concretely or abstractly by determining if the person is talking about either a specific time in the past or talk about *right now,* where a named person or thing did something. If you listen to this person for up to 30 minutes, you will know if they are abstract or concrete in general.

In order to effectively influence the action of these types, a leader must adjust their speech. While this may look like a futile effort in pandering, instead, adjusting speech is an acceptance that people require different conditions to thrive.

Concrete persons require being told in clear terms what exactly they need to do when it needs to be done and the specific metrics that they will be measured with. Without this specific language, the concrete person will idle or do something else.

Influencing abstract persons requires appealing to either their sense of values and morality or their sense of greater utility. Instead of telling them *specifically* what to do, abstract types are influenced by stating, *in general*, what needs doing or what is missing. Allowing them the person instead to fill in the blanks.

Those who fail to bridge "concrete or abstract" communication with those whom they encounter will find frustration and miss their opportunity to influence or receive the queues for how to influence the person.

Is your purpose cooperation or utility?

Some people are entirely focused on cooperation. Their largest driving purpose is to be accepted by others or be in alignment with how the group believes.

The act of cooperation is the activity of taking turns and working together without necessarily focusing on which ideas or personal capabilities are better. Cooperative people, whether abstract or concrete, evaluate others by how much they are willing to work with them. You might hear something like:

"I don't like those people at all; every time I talk to them, they won't help me out."

Cooperative types, along with concrete types, make up the majority of people. Because cooperative people operate in the world by dealing in "to and from others", they become the embodiment of the ideas, habits, and morality of those around them. They are often the greatest product of their environment.

Influence Tip: Influencing Cooperative Types

Leaders influence cooperative types by performing actions for the other person, which can be as simple as listening to them. Since cooperative types are sensitive to people helping them, it is often the case that little deeds go a long way in influence.

Others are focused entirely on utility. For these people, the usefulness of everything is the most important aspect of concern, rather than its elements of cooperation. "This way of doing it is actually faster." Or "this is a better tool because it's easier to do the work." Contrast this with the cooperative person, who will select tools for reasons such as "the company is well known."

Utility types evaluate others by their competence and ability to get work accomplished well.

When a utility type of person encounters a person or team that doesn't help them out, they might say:

"I didn't need them anyway. I figured it out on my own."

Influence Tip: Influencing Utility Types

Leaders influence utility types by improving their abilities and focusing on getting things accomplished. Utility-minded people are relatively content not having their ideas be adopted so long as the idea adopted is the best idea for the situation. However, it is often from these utility-minded people where the best functional ideas come from. A leader looking at the whole will know when that is.

For both of these types of people, cooperation and utility it is a statement about purpose. What is the purpose of a thing or a person? Cooperative people behave as though making a more cohesive group is the most important purpose in life, while the utility person behaves as though the functional capability of the people is the most important. One should not underestimate how important this distinction is, as it affects every bit of how these people are influenced.

While the communicative barrier between the concrete and abstract speaker causes confusion and frustration when not addressed, the barrier of purpose between cooperation and utility is much more severe. Failing to communicate across cooperative and utility boundaries creates **animosity, hatred, and collapse.**

An effective leader knows that earning influence with either person requires adjusting the behavior and focuses. While it can be an ongoing struggle to communicate with some people, it is necessary to *subdue* your own lashing out due to a mismatch in purpose.

If you combine Utility and Cooperation with Concrete and Abstract, you get four types of people:

1. Concrete Cooperative
2. Concrete Utility
3. Abstract Cooperative
4. Abstract Utility

Consider for a moment how different these people really are. Each day, how they see things in the world and the language that they use are completely different. Now consider they have spent their entire lives as these four diverse types.

> Leaders must understand the differences in people
> to avoid needless frustration and animosity while
> keeping clear communications and aligning people
> with a purpose fit for *them.*

CHAPTER 23

Treat Everyone the Same

While people are different in profound ways, people are still the same. There are many attributes that nearly everyone shares, enabling certain actions of influence to be applicable across all temperaments and personalities. Discovering these common attributes gives leaders the ability to manage earning influence even in complex environments.

Of course, every person needs water, food, sleep, shelter, and energy to stay alive, but there are much deeper aspects that make up the psychological makeup of a person.

Dale Carnegie points out in *How to Win Friends and Influence People*, "Remember that a person's name is to that person the sweetest and most important sound in any language." This quote is a testament to both the infatuation with-self, but also that most people are quite similar.

Take, for example, having a purpose.

People need to feel as though they have a purpose. Meaning, there is something specific that their life is focused around that "has value." Whether or not it is true that someone can "have a purpose" is irrelevant to the fact that people *believe* they need to have one, and without it, they languish. People, especially those who are healthy, will seek out physical and mental clues to help answer "what is the purpose of my life?" Those souls who consciously or subconsciously ask this question and *don't* have an answer can often begin living a destructive lifestyle "crying out for help."

Humans need purpose and, without it, will seek purpose until their dying days. *This is important for influence because helping a person find their purpose earns influence.*

How People Are Similar

The following is a non-exhaustive list of factors that make people similar:

- Everyone loves people who consistently lift them up.
- People need a person who will listen to their problems and not necessarily try to solve them.
- People love those who believe in them, even when they do not believe in themselves.
- People desire to be valuable.
- People desire for efforts to be easy and rewards to be big.
- People need to believe there is a future and they have a place in it.
- People languish without clear direction and purpose.

How to use and not use similarities in people

Every similarity that has been listed can be used to earn influence with others. Given that all people have these attributes, then messages and actions can be crafted to suit each person based on them. But remember, everyone is also different, so how one does it is also very different.

Consider a person who is a concrete; that is, they value what they can physically see, touch, or smell rather than what is imagined. When encouraging and lifting these people up, one should look at using physical means, such as pats on the back and praise about the clothes they are wearing or things they own. For some people, this seems awkward, yet; *this can be what that person needs.*

For comparison, abstract people that need encouragement can be lifted by pointing out not only how far they have come but rather where they are going and praising their ingenuity or foresight. Not that these types don't like physical encouragement, they very well may, but these are starting points in understanding that people need encouragement; just how it's done at the individual level can vary greatly.

Avoid pointing out "sameness" or treating people "the same"

While there are some types of people who are looking to be "normal", many people do not like to be lumped into a category or be reduced to "being like everyone else." The strangeness of realizing that everyone is the same is knowing that many attributes about people *are* indeed the same, *yet* most don't want to be accepted as the same. After all, if they are the same as with someone else, then they are replaceable, right? How can you be valuable if somebody could replace you?

Unless one knows who they are speaking with, it is best to avoid treating everyone the same. While some people really demand that everybody be treated equally, the vast majority of people do not like this idea.

Never forget leadership is influencing people into action, not necessarily embodying ideals such as "equality". Consider instead, continually asking the following questions: "what is necessary to assist the people in moving forward." This question will help identify what actions are needed and what is blocking those actions. Using the shortlist of "how people are the same" is an easy way to figure out actions even when you don't know what to do.

> Leaders should continue to identify the common
> areas where nearly all people can be influenced.
> As they are identified, they should be worked
> into the personality. Doing so will cause even
> unconscious actions to earn influence consistently.

CHAPTER 24

Cultivate Trust and Belief

When people want something in life, how do they know if what they are doing will give them what they want?

If they want a high quality of life, how do they know if college is a good choice?

How does the writer of this book *know* that the publishing of this book will accomplish its intended mission by being created?

While people can build plans, strategies, and intent, ultimately, nobody knows if the actions they take will be guaranteed to bring them what they want. Instead, people do actions **because they believe them to be true.**

> Those who take action have faith that their
> actions will bring them what they intend, and
> if it fails to work perfectly, they believe in
> themselves enough to know what to try next.

Like faith, belief goes far beyond the hallowed grounds of churches, religion, and superstition. The formation of belief is critical towards action. Belief comes *before* action. One has to believe that an action has a good chance of having its intended consequence in order to take that action.

Ask yourself, if you did not believe an action would work, would you do it in the first place?

Some might answer, "to see what would happen." But even in that case, there is the belief that by doing the action, there will be an interesting result. Even when we act just to see what happens, we have a belief that something will happen and that something is worth observing.

Even Math and Physics is a Belief

Even the sciences have the inescapable human quality of belief before action.

People believe that by using the "tricks" and "gotchas" found in mathematical relations, they can discover new possibilities in the world. In fact, James Clerk Maxwell, a famous scientist, **did this very thing.**

Sometime near 1862, James Clerk Maxwell predicted the existence of radio waves through equations he was working on tying electricity to magnetism. Through the process of manipulating his calculus equations, he was able to predict the existence of radio waves. By discovering that radio waves were in a direct relationship with light, he began the process of trying to manifest that into reality.

Twenty years later, following Maxwell, Heinrich Rudolf Hertz used rapid variations in electrical current to create radio waves. Twenty more years later, Italian inventor, Guglielmo Marconi was able to transmit a wireless "S" character from England to Newfoundland.

All of this was a derivative of the following **beliefs:**

1. Mathematical relationships, no matter how quirky, have a connection to reality.

2. The scientist can know *how* the mathematical relationships map to reality.

3. Performing an experiment using a given set of instruments maps both to the mathematical relationships being tested, and the results are congruent with the believed map of reality.

Are these statements universally true?
No. Beliefs can turn out to be false.

For every scientific experiment that breaks ground, there is an untold number of experiments that do not. While every failure provides some added wisdom, experiments can also yield unexpected results to include spurious results or results that are not what is being tested.

None of this matters because **belief** is a requirement for action, and all of these scientists had beliefs that drove them in the directions that they chose. All scientists had to push through many setbacks in the pursuit of their beliefs.

In the spirit of understanding beliefs, ask yourself, why did I tell you a story about three scientists and the origin of radio waves?

Because *I believe* that it's a convincing enough example that it will make *you believe* in the power of *belief.*

People are willing to do the wrong thing for themselves and others because their beliefs are bad. People believe that making safe choices keeps them safe.

If every action originates from a belief that a person holds to be true, then every bad action comes from a bad belief. And this is why understanding belief matters...

In order to influence someone, they must believe you're there to help them.

In order to compel someone to follow you, they must believe that following behind you is a faster way to getting what they want. What is it that the person in front of you believes is valuable? Is it a "cause"? Is it to help their family?

As leaders progress through life, they must master belief. Leaders must be able to operate in a person's belief systems. Leaders who seek to learn and understand what other people believe will know how to earn influence and where it can be expended well. Those who do not learn the belief systems of others at best will poorly influence and, at worse, create enemies.

CHAPTER 25

Manage Habits

Generally, do you like to sit, or do you like to stand? Why?

Are you the kind of person who tends to money or spends money? Why?

Do you practice any arts such as music or exercise daily? Why?

Other than a few distinct cases, the reason one does or doesn't do any of these falls squarely on habits.

A person's habits shape everything about them.

There is the saying that you cannot teach an old dog new tricks. This, like every other one-line statement, is only partially the story. In reality, "old dogs" often have *many* **habits** that need to be broken in order to learn new tricks.

Habits develop over time as we make and follow through with small decisions that produce some sort of "positive effect". We can get entertainment, satisfaction, self-identity, and even the thrill of taboo. As we follow through with those actions, we bring them into our being; thus, habits are formed.

Trajectories of a person change when habits are reformed.

Depending on which habits we adopt will determine what outputs we produce. The following are but a few habits and their results:

Habits of productivity beget a life of abundance. Habits of sloth beget a life of meager resources.

Habits of intention beget a life of direction, with rich accomplishment. Habits of spontaneity beget a life shallowness and trivial rewards.

Habits of taking small action, beget the chance for small rewards. Habits of taking large action, beget the chance for large rewards. Even luck itself is determined by your habits.

If you want a person to behave differently, consistently, they have to begin systematically breaking down their habits by improving their thinking and acting.

Influence Tip: Work with Strengths

Be careful in considering to take on changing a person. It is far better to work with people on their strengths and learn how to mitigate their weaknesses. Changing people is a complex, full topic that deserves its own book. For this purpose, know that people can *only* change when they've changed their habits. If a leader decides to spend more time around a person, the other person's habits will change. Just by being themselves, a leader will influence the habits of others.

Habits are reinforced by other habits

What makes these habits stick are habits of reinforcement. Like cement pouring around a mold, habits that reinforce keep us in the shape that we are now. These habits, too, are created every day.

How many habits are going on without you observing them? Think of your own habits occurring in private, away from the view of others. Do these habits have any impact on how you perform in public? Do these private habits have any impact on your confidence in public?

Unquestioned habits can have complete domination over life

In the year 2020, one of the largest habits is to do "digital research" instead of personal experience. The ease at being able to reach at arm's length for "all the information in the world" has tempted people to abdicate experience for the described experiences of others.

"Where should we eat?"

"How do we get there?"

As digital devices seem to have "all the easy answers", is it any wonder why people have adopted multi-layered habits based around them? The result of which is their face is regularly pointed at a screen and readily adopt the ideas that come from it.

> Leaders must acknowledge the power of habits and discover their own habits and the habits of others. Helping to make others aware of their habits gives them a chance to intentionally choose *better* habits and begin the process of personal transformation. Leaders ought to consider investing the time in learning how to create habits intentionally so they can lead others to do the same.

CHAPTER 26

Shape the Environment, Life Will Adapt

One of the most peculiar features of life is that it changes. Life will change what it does from day to day and moment to moment if necessary. But why?

Life responds to changing environments.

Everywhere around you, all lifeforms, whether it is a tree, a squirrel, a fox, a beaver, fescue grass, or a spider in your house, are responding and changing to their environment. There is no need to go into esoteric sciences such as Darwinism in order to understand this, as it is plainly observable.

Trees bend into shapes based on dominant winds.

Squirrels, an animal known for running from humans, in some areas allow humans to come so close that they can almost be touched.

Black widows cannot be found in busy areas, but when light is gone, and movement stops, they begin to build their nests.

It is these environments that create the conditions for the situation, where some realities are favored over others.

Every human lives within an environment.

Because of the complexity of human lives, the human environment is filled with not only other people but ideas, systems, and if they are lucky, at least a tiny bit of nature.

This environment shapes and molds *nearly* every aspect of the person, from what they wear to what they become.

In certain environments, people grow up healthy, work well with others, create stability, have care and concern not just for humans but all creatures while simultaneously wielding power, justly and judiciously. In other environments, people become crooked, are hostile to others, create instability, focus on themselves and attempt to gain power through desperate force and coercion.

Environments shape what people focus on, what their problems are, and size and character of their circles of concern and influence. It tells them whether they are valued or not. It shows a person if there is a future for them or a wasted life.

There is no question to the importance of knowing that humans live within "a context" and operate from a day-to-day basis with this in mind.

Begin Studying Environments

Since environments play such an integral role in influence, leaders need to understand where they are and what they are stepping into. As an environment's characteristics are gathered, opportunities present themselves that can be used to uniquely influence people into action. These opportunities can then be stitched together to build a plan for the future.

As you examine environments, remember that **everything** makes up this environment, whether it is the size of a dwelling, junk mail and trash scattered on horizontal surfaces, the social dynamics among people who occupy the environment, and even the acknowledged history of the area.

Luxury causes people to lose their zeal for life.

Cramped living quarters tell people, "they're small."

Clutter, erroneously, reminds people that they do not have enough time nor resources.

Influence Tip: Looks can be deceiving

Humans are exceptionally complex creatures, and it's not always obvious from the physical looks what is really happening. An example is when a person owns *a lot* of things. One might think that this person is filled with abundance, but unless they have the habit of giving to others, it's more likely they have a fear of not having enough. This message is reinforced by the environment around them.

> When left unchecked, stagnant environments become standard and regularized. Overtime, mediocrity then embeds into the unconsciousness of the mind.

The following are a few aspects to evaluate an environment:

1. Are people actively improving their skills? Is there a culture of growth?

2. Do people routinely point the finger away from themselves when things go wrong? Is there a culture of excuse-making rather than responsibility-taking?

3. Are the people going anywhere? Is there a *specific* future ahead of them?

4. Do the people know each other well enough to know what influences each other, especially if asked?

5. Does the environment operate using force regularly, or is there encouragement?

When the above aspects are low, leadership is missing.

In situations where leadership is missing, commonly known as a leadership vacuum, there is stagnation, crumbling social connections, and a low resiliency in people.

In contrast, when the above aspects are in abundance, there is reinforcement among people, you can feel the momentum of the environment going somewhere, and life is supportive.

> Know that environment sculpting never ends.
> Environments are always changing, if not by
> you, then by degrading over time, converting
> excellence into mediocrity.

Influence Tip: Lead in Difficult Environments

It is much "easier" to lead in environments where influence is flowing and present. In many ways, they are on autopilot. However, this is not where leadership is needed most. It is in the environments of challenge. Those who influence in easy environments will never know if the results are from their actions or from the environment itself. The opposite is said for those who work in challenging areas.

The Leader Shapes an Environment by Shaping Themselves First

Now we can accept the truth about an environment. The leader *is* the environment. The environment is the leader. People adopt the habits and behaviors of the leaders.

> Are you aware that *your habits and behaviors* rub
> off on others? Do you take personal responsibility
> for the flaws of others?

In order to shape the environment, the leader needs to first shape themselves. *Each* person is critical to shaping the environment, so the leader needs to be the most shaped.

The Leader Sets the Tone

The way this works is very simple. What is presented here is not magic. I am not saying that every time you tickle your nose, everyone around you will tickle theirs. What *I am* saying is that the leader's actions, especially the larger they are, have a profound impact on the environment around them.

People regularly perform actions simply because they are influenced by the leader's own behavior. In the bizarre world of corporations, this is called "corporate culture."

When people like and respect you, they adopt behaviors that are similar to yours because they want that certain "something" that you possess. Confidence begets more confidence. **This is why choosing your own actions is of high importance for a leader.**

The leader shows what is permissible or not. If a leader leaves trash lying around, then trash will begin to be left around. If the leader accumulates stuff, people will begin accumulating. **If you do actions without informing anyone that you are performing them, do not be surprised when others start doing "their own thing" as well.**

This truth is so pervasive it is difficult to describe how vast and how far it goes. A look into organizations shows this truth.

In offices and workplaces where praise is absent, it's because the leader never praises.

In organizations where there are pockets of mediocrity and decay that are overlooked, it's because the leaders do not have a habit of inspecting the details.

In homes where parents claim that children need to know more about nature but never step outside themselves, their children will grow to say one thing but do another.

Organizations where people aggressively grab for control, it's because the leaders are continually trying to control how everything is done.

As "the leader" develops and changes over time you can see that they begin to see the world differently by the changing effects within the organization. Leaders begin communicating this new profound belief to those who are following them.

As a result of their "epiphanies", the leaders act differently and communicate differently. People will shift their words because the leader shifts their words. People will shift their behaviors because the leader has shifted his behaviors. It takes time, but eventually, followers get on board with what the leaders are doing.

A healthy leader evolves their behavior through better self-awareness and environmental awareness.

Leaders have no choice but to accept the reality that what they do matters and has an impact. **This truth should be taught to others as well.**

You Need to Decide, Live with the Decision and Communicate It to Others

You need to determine what exactly you want your environment to be. You need to make the determination, **now** how others ought to *talk with each other and talk with you.* These decisions are needed now so *you can begin doing it.*

Decisions are lived by the leader first. Just do it.

In order to reinforce this decision, you need to immediately begin shaping the environment to help reinforce this. By doing so, the world helps **YOU** live by this decision.

Should people talk kindly to each other?

Start talking kindly to others, and when people do not talk kindly to you, **plainly state it to them that you believe people should speak kindly with each other.** *Do so without frustration, with full confidence, and without concern for any response by them.*

Do not get mired in the fact that others might be bothered by your determinations in this regard. Change is uncomfortable. **But remember, people adapt to their environment, and you are part of their environment.** Consider for a moment that if it is the kind of change that **needs to happen,** then the choice is really simple.

CHAPTER 27

Lean into Leadership Hierarchies

Before explaining a powerful phenomenon, it is necessary to make a declaration. The ideas surrounding the organizing of humans within the 20th and 21st centuries have become so incredibly convoluted it is no wonder there is crisis after crisis. Rather than dwell on invented and difficult to prove political abstractions, let's discuss the natural organization of humans by their relationships as a set of tiers. An organization called a "hierarchy."

A hierarchy is an organization of humans based on **tiers of relationships**. If one person is influencing a second person, that is one-tier. If the second person then influences a third person, that is a second tier. And so on. As the first person begins influencing the second, influence trickles to the next as the second person picks up the habits, ideas, and behaviors of the first leader. Without even knowing it, the third person begins to take on behaviors that originally stemmed from the first person. This is how cultures are created and how people begin to gain an identity as a group.

Without trying to prove anything complicated, this is an obvious example of how real-life relationships work. It is not necessary to use political, academic, or media theories to demonstrate this.

While it is common to view this situation as a pyramid, it often implies there is more going on than there is. Instead, consider the arrangement of concentric circles. Let's look at these in a series of pictures.

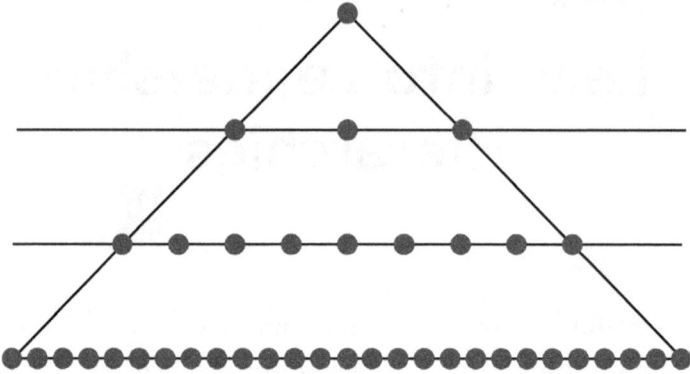

A typical, but unhelpful view of a natural hierarchy.

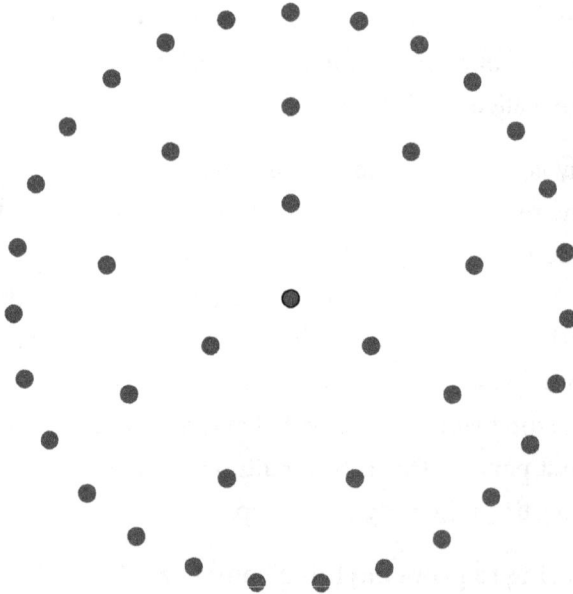

Consider for a moment, an organized group of people.

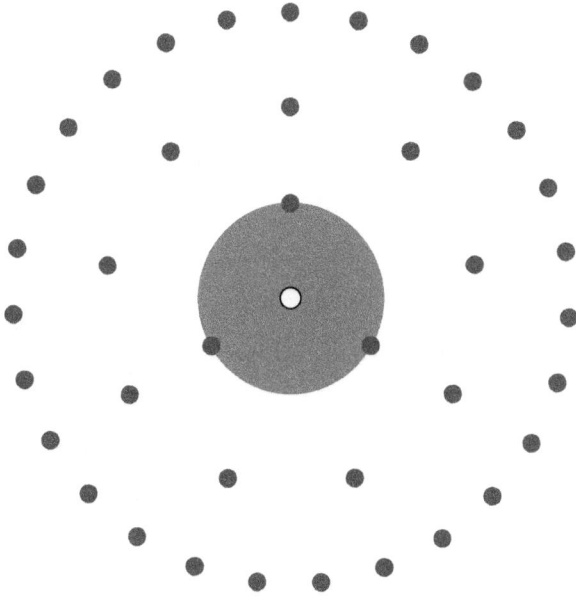

Where the center person begins influencing three people around themselves.

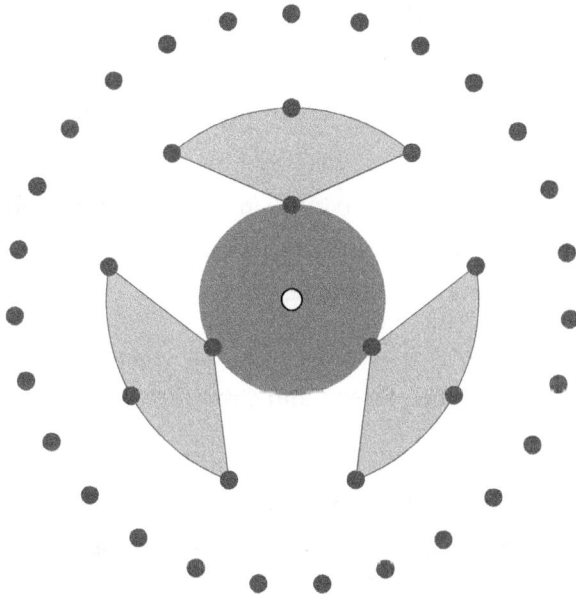

And then those persons begin influencing three more.

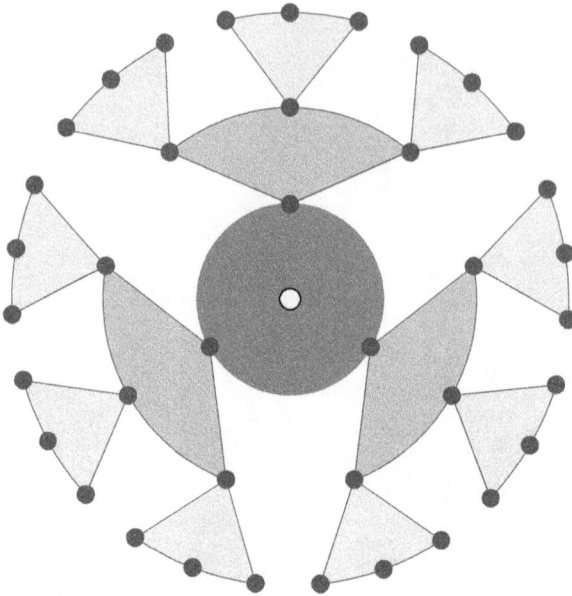

*And then those three influence three more people themselves.
You can see that the original person has the ability to influence
36 people just by influencing three. Whether this is intentional or
not is irrelevant. What is true is that one person has the ability to
influence many by influencing only a few.*

The natural tier creation of relationships is the way hierarchies natu-rally evolve around a leader. This is not by some systemic design, but by the truth that it's difficult to build ***highly influential relationships*** with people; therefore, **multiple leaders** are always necessary for any endeavor larger than 1 or 3 people.

Note: The complexity of relationships can create not-so-simplified hierarchies where some of tier 3 and 4 may be directly influenced by others in tier 1, 2, or 3.

Consider developing strong functional relationships with approx-imately three people, and encourage those people to lead others.

This "three-person leadership" method is utilized the world over, sometimes intentionally and often by accident. The military uses it, and even business tycoons use it. This method is most commonly utilized by military organizations to organize their troops.

1. A fire team is three people and one fire squad leader.
2. A squad is three fire teams and one squad leader.
3. A platoon is three squads with one platoon leader.
4. A company is three platoons and one company commander.
5. A battalion is three companies and one battalion commander.
6. A regiment is three battalions and one regimental commander.
7. A division is three regiments and one division commander.
8. A corps is three divisions and a corps commander.
9. An army is three corps and one army commander.

If the military organizes their entire operations using this pattern of three people to one person, doesn't it make sense to take this pattern seriously? You may be asking, "Why three people to a leader? "

It is too difficult to *effectively* manage any more than three people at a time; however, through hierarchies, it's possible to amplify influence.

Imagine You Are Leading

Imagine you have an organization where you are in *the* lead role. Imagine that this organization has multiple layers of hierarchy. There are three people who you directly influence, and those three people directly influence three others each. Now imagine there are new people who come into the organization at the outer-most rings.

In order to influence those who just joined, you decide to influence your three people. They begin influencing their three people, who will then begin influencing the new people to the organization.

You, as the leader of the organization, will be raised up because all of the other leaders will convey information, stories, and admiration about **you** to the new people. From the moment they arrive, they will have a *very* heightened picture of who you are. **Yet you are still you, and nothing has changed.**

Imagine you get off your high horse for a moment at being the leader and *briefly* interact with the newest people.

This is where odd behavior begins to happen that you could never experience outside of this arrangement.

People you don't know that you have never physically done anything directly for will begin to honor you. They have a high chance of feeling emotional effects in your presence, such as tingly sensations throughout their body and the feeling of being unable to speak.

Just a moment before you showed up, these new people were feeling just fine, and all of a sudden, they now have heightened alertness and the need to keep their mouths closed.

If you have good enough character, you will decide to perform a small act of generosity by honoring them and their decision to join with you. Through performing such an insignificant act that others might normally take for granted, you lift them dramatically to newer heights. **With at least one of them, it is likely that you earned a very high level of dedication to you *personally,* giving all your future actions a much higher influence with them.**

These kinds of actions, taken at the right times, cause entire organizations to float higher and gain cohesion.

It is very important to take in what is going on in this "imaginary" story. Imagine you walked into a grocery store and encountered these same new people; except they were not part of your organization and had never heard of you. They are likely to feel no emotions in your presence and might be likely to ignore you even exist. Yet, just by being influenced by others within your organization, a completely different situation occurs.

It is the **multiple layers of influence** that amplify the effects of even the simplest encounter.

> It's important that leaders understand that if, or rather when, they get in this situation, they know what to do. Your job is to influence, lead, and raise these people higher. Make no mistake, the influencing effect on people within hierarchies is very real.

CHAPTER 28

Use Self-Infatuation to Earn Influence

The only way on earth to influence other people is to talk about what they want and show them how to get it.

—Dale Carnegie in
How to Win Friends and Influence People

Whether it is their ideas, opinions, recommendations, or even their own faults, everyone cannot get enough of themselves. The implications of this demonstrate that influence comes from engaging with what another person cares about. If a want-a-be leader tries to influence using ideas and actions that another person does not care about, there will be no influence. If you'd like to prove this maxim to yourself, here is an observation.

Begin a conversation with a person where the focus is on something that relates to the person, such as a recent event they experienced. After finishing this conversation change the topic to an experience that you had personally that they did not participate in. Make no excessive attempts to entertain; just provide the facts. Compare the enthusiasm that the person has for the two topics.

Do they ask many questions? Do they really dig into the topic? Would they carry on the conversation without you there at all?

Unless the topic was unbelievably sensational, your topic will make no mark at all. In fact, you talking about this topic consumes just a little bit of your influence since you are compelling the person to listen to you, especially about a topic they don't care about.

What you will find is the person loves to tell you their own personal opinions, personal observations, personal thoughts, or personal experiences through a story.

Influence Tip: Keeping someone's attention

If you are trying to communicate with a person, and find that the other person is starting to drift off and no longer paying attention, immediately connect the topic to the other person. An example is asking, "what do you think about this?" You can stay on the primary topic; just change gears so that the other person's feelings, thoughts, etc., are now able to be expressed. *Like magic*, the person will pop into place excited.

Skilled conversationalists know-how to re-direct back to the other person

A person who is skilled in conversation knows and understands this desire for people to talk about themselves. A dialogue is a discussion that results in a back and forth between people. This back and forth requires that each person turn over the baton of talking about themselves. A person who understands conversation **intentionally** hands over the baton to the other person, giving them room to speak about themselves.

Those who are not focused on this principle decide to take the baton and share information that they already know about themselves. As a result, missing an opportunity to discover about the other person and have the chance to flow them in the direction they might want them to go.

Leaders ask about others.

Leaders understand that being interested in others creates a draw to them. While a conversationalist is good at keeping a conversation flowing back and forth, a leader keeps turning the conversation back over to others whom they want to hear from. Even if a leader speaks, they ask others what they think about what they've said. A leader is seeking to gain valuable insights when questions are asked. Each time the baton is passed back over, the leader earns influence. The leader is giving, **through actions**, that they are interested in the other person.

People are influenced by those who are interested in them. Watch the behavior of any newly married couple if you have doubts.

Even your frustrations are all about you.

Throughout life, you will notice that people can often lash out at you; even seemingly out of nowhere. You may even find that at times people will talk bad about you to others and dislike things that you are doing.

If you still have not fully internalized that people are infatuated with themselves, you will miss the understanding that their frustrations are really statements about themselves. Everything is a reflection based on their current values and mental framing.

Simply put, when others lash out or talk negatively about people, it comes from their own self-focused, internal feelings.

Consider for a moment that negativity is a poison.

Have you ever noticed that people who harbor ideas that are poisonous feel desperate to get them out? If you were bit by a creature and poisoned, wouldn't you want the poison to somehow be sucked out of you?

> *"A person who is low in other people, is low in themselves."*
> —John Maxwell

People who are low in themselves feel better and comforted by pointing to the flaws of other individuals. By pointing out failures, they are implicitly saying how they are better. This action of raising themselves up by lowering others actually prevents them from earning long-term self-worth because they are not higher; everyone else is just lower.

Real self-worth is obtained by overcoming adversities and achieving desires, *NOT* by lowering others.

> *"Hurt people, hurt people."*
>
> —John Maxwell

Overcoming adversities and achieving desires gives a person a sense of control and mastery, rather than living at the whims of the universe. Instead, like eating junk food, a person who trashes others becomes momentarily satiated by the act of knocking down the gentle straw men in their life. No real problems are solvable by knocking down paper targets.

Poisonous feelings always boil back to frustrations with oneself.

People who are frustrated feel incapable of influencing and changing the environment around them. Their ultimate focus is on their inability to change what they see as violations of their value systems. This behavior will fall on your doorstep.

The following statement requires a bit of fine line caution, ***but the truth is worth saying to its absolute fullest.***

If you take other people's poison personally, as in you mistake it to be about you personally, in *any way*, **even if it is directed at you personally**, you will acerbate their sickness.

This doesn't mean ignore or don't listen to a person lashing out at you, but consider for a moment that such passionate statements might reach too far or are out of alignment with what is true universally.

You must never forget that it's someone's internal focus that creates frustrations and poisonous beliefs.

It is **their own personal fear that is the origin**, which is then is **rationalized and externalized out into the world**. Those who are strong deal with these emotions differently, such as maneuvering around them or becoming vulnerable by seeking assistance from others.

Influence Tip: Getting the other person to speak

Sometimes just stroking a mustache, looking them in the eye, and appearing to be pondering what they're saying, is all that is necessary for enabling someone to vent their negative emotions. If you don't know what to do, consider doing nothing and just "being there." Don't engage with the content being said whatsoever, just the person saying it. Weirdly enough, it works.

If someone is blaring their frustrations out on you, it is recommended to hear their frustrations out, take notes for considerations on your own personal tactics and strategies, and then move forward without dwelling on them.

> Just because a person is frustrated
> doesn't mean it's a bad situation.

Growth requires overcoming frustrations. If self-worth is earned by overcoming adversities and achieving one's desires, then overcoming frustration **must** be part of life. If you happen to be the one who causes the frustrations in others in pursuit of a higher purpose, then so be it. Those who engage too deeply in others' frustrations guarantee to adopt their frustrations as their own.

> The infatuation with oneself is the
> root of all suffering.

There is no further evidence needed for how far infatuation with self goes than looking at the modern consumer. The modern consumer evaluates all of human existence based on the products consumed.

A very toxic, yet common, consumer acts as though they **never believe** they have enough products to consume. These individuals tend to always point to "the rich" that they believe consume more and then believe that those who consume less suffer.

Influence Tip: Influence by Frustrating

Have no fears when you are in the mix of frustrating people. If you have the right heart about it, you are patient, methodical, and heavy on listening; you have nothing to worry about. Practice becoming invulnerable. (See Internalize Being Invulnerable) If you have no fears while having hard conversations, you keep the discussion objective, clear and productive. Even the most sensitive people are willing to hear direct criticism **if** you can handle the dance that goes with it. As long as you embody the mission *and ensure that they know that you believe they do too*, they'll never turn away. **Fear not!**

No, it is them who are suffering.

It is *their* internal focus and how they frame the world in terms of consumption that brings suffering. This is what they feel internally that is then externalized onto the world. These same people advocate that governments ought to use resources and force to intervene in other cultures' existence.

In the end, suffering is another manifestation of the inward focus of a person. **To make it crystal clear, a person cannot be influenced without communicating directly with what *they* care about: their values, their opinions, their viewpoints, etc.**

The communication component of leadership is being able to see what a person sees as best as is possible and then bridge the gap from there to where you are trying to take them.

It does not matter what your arguments are; you will not overcome a person's feelings with them. The only way you can overcome a person's issues is by focusing on connecting with the values of the other person.

In plain language, if a person is stuck inside themselves, they're likely going to feel a lot of pain. There are at least two ways to pull them out of themselves.

Two Ways to Get Someone Unstuck

1. Ask them to share about themselves

The first is you have to jump into their world and speak using what they value but lead them out. The easiest way to do this is by getting them to share about themselves and then leading them out by asking questions.

When you ask someone what they think or believe, it gives people energy. The reason is very simple.

By asking about a person, it is a 100% sure way to know that you must care about them, even if it's a little. You give them a platform for existence that the world may not be providing. The default state of affairs is people speak right past each other. With no platform, people are never sure if their statements had an impact on a listener. As a result, more and more sensational things get said.

Why do you think that media has become so over-the-top dramatic and sensational in the 21st century? Nobody's listening, just projecting.

By leaders giving others the power to talk about their position or point of view, the "self" is allowed to come out in a safe, controlled, and productive way: a surefire way to earn influence.

> ## Influence Tip: Building report with Questions
> Questions and listening are your friend. The more you can keep *your*self out of this situation, the better.

This approach is a solid way to build rapport with a person, which is a fancy way of saying you will earn influence by yielding over your attention and time.

2. Get them to do something productive.

Getting someone to move physically to overcome an issue is a maneuvering tactic that works. Instead of directly addressing someone's frustrations, leaders can ignore the content and go straight to the core. What's the real issue?

Low self-worth, coming from not doing anything productive.

Never forget that people turn internally focused because they have uncertainty and negative feelings. This is a low productivity state because their personal needs and desires, which are at the whims of their internal emotions, come over the needs and desires of everything else. It is difficult for this kind of person to be present for the external world and the needs of others. This person has the feeling that everything else is taking away from *them*.

Getting moving and doing positive things, even if it's going through the motions at first, can change that.

This is why exercise can be such an important component of a healthy lifestyle. Through a little bit of exercise or physical labor, you earn a sense of life mastery.

While maneuvering around frustration issues by getting a person to be productive does not earn you a lot of influence, it does have the other person's best needs in mind.

Remember this chapter applies to you.

You are a person too. You are most infatuated with your ideas, your direction, and the way that you think. Be careful getting sucked into talking about yourself and instead find safe avenues for expressing yourself without it affecting you detrimentally.

Know that there is no satiation with this infatuation. The more you talk about yourself, the more you will want to do it.

Continually train yourself to resist the *need* to take up the oxygen in the room, especially with elements that add little to no value to others.

As you grow, you *ought* to feel significantly less need for filler. Now you can provide support, guidance and the critical service of a listening ear that will actually hear you out.

> The better we can navigate the human
> component, which demands selfish creature needs,
> the better. Time is precious.

Influence Tip: Being production yourself

As you become good at listening to others, you may consider the need to create a hide-a-way area where you can get work done privately. Interruptions will be constant, and people will often seek you out because **you actually listen**. Waking up early is also often a requirement for getting in private work time.

CHAPTER 29

Help Others Obtain Power

Conscious leaders ought to consider how much complexity exists. The understanding of the good use of power is one; another is walking the path to victory while staying away from the pitfalls that inevitably encroach around every step.

> People want to know someone who is powerful, so they can use them as tools to get what they desire.

The fact that someone *believes* that someone has power is indicative that they believe that person can help them. This "powerful person" has power because others yield it over to them.

Have you ever noticed people will wait around for a hero to come and save them from whatever stagnant life situation they find themselves in?

Have you also heard people say, "somebody ought to do something about… ."?

These types of statements demonstrate how a person believes that there are powerful people out there, and "if only" that person swooped down, things would be better for them. If you listen and observe people carefully, you might find this belief is pervasive in human thoughts and desires. This inner desire is part of why influence is effective, but there is an issue.

Listen carefully to the following unexpected turn. It is perhaps one of the most important sub-points in this entire text.

You must resist doing everything for everyone.
This is not leadership.

Yes, performing actions is a requirement for earning influence. Yes, one ought to listen to others regularly and seek to solve problems.

But becoming the powerful person that everyone taps to be *their* powerful person is NOT leadership.

Leadership is about compelling *others* to solve problems. Every time someone gets you to solve **their** problem for them, you receive power from the loss of their own.

The person who does everything for everyone becomes the person who robs everyone of their ability to get to a better life. This person just reinforces the delusion that they have no power.

Consider when you listen to people ask things of you of what kind of problems these are and their origins. Most problems that others will ask you to solve are problems of their own creation. These problems, personal problems, ones in which they ought to have the power to solve. Most often, but not always, these problems fall into the realm of "**smaller than oneself**" meaning, they are not problems that affect groups of people but problems that affect one's own individual needs and desires.

Examine the situation of over-parenting

"Mom!!!! I want milk!"

This phrase, uttered by many children young and old, is a testament to over-parenting. In nearly every one of these situations, the child is perfectly capable of gathering and pouring their own beverage yet wants the parent to do it for them. These requests are often subtle, and yet the ramifications over time are clear.

By the year 2020, the impact of super-hero parenting are as follows:

1. **Adults who can't make eye contact with others** – They have minimal ability to connect with others. They are weak and supple prey.

2. **Adults with XYZ syndrome/disease/excuse** – Just because people don't fit the "perfect" systemic mold doesn't mean they ought to be held back forever by excuses. Not to mention cattle for industrial poisons.

3. **Adults who feel entitled to the services of others** – They demand the products and services of the world and other people. "Free" is best, rather than earned.

4. **Adults who are political activists.** – Pawns are used because of their toxic belief that someone else is responsible for solving their problems.

5. **Adults who cannot regulate their emotions** – Every time their emotions pop up, nobody helped them handle their emotions. Instead, just providing more stuff to quiet them. Instead, these "adults" associate emotions with things and servants.

If This Isn't Compelling Enough, Consider What Will Happen to You Personally

If you decide to take the path of solving everyone's problems, if you decide to join the Greek gods and become Atlas, you will earn what befalls such a person.

You will receive everyone's problems.

All responsibility will be turned over to you. Success and failure, to include perceptions of both. Everything will require your attention to go forward. At first, this feels great. You will feel as though you're steering your destiny! Although over time, its frustration will set in. Everything begins to accelerate.

Eventually, you can no longer steer destiny and get mired in the weeds.

You'll run into the fact there is simply too much to do that a single person cannot do it all. Since no one around you has built up the muscles to handle setbacks, everyone will blame you for the tiniest failures. People will leave your side, in droves, even if you've done much for them, because it's clear you're not so powerful after all.

If you get into this situation, your reality will be confused. You might even come to believe that the people are in error.

> These are not the views of a person who is
> leading. These are the views of an individual who
> is frustrated and playing the "woe is me" game.

What a leader does is see the potential in others and guide them to the path of personal and shared victory.

A leader *knows* that people have *immense* potential and constantly seeks to spark its emergence. In order to do that, leaders must be able to maneuver and even gain a bit of cunning to manifest this emergence. Real leaders, those who live and die by influence, know that the keys to victory are always **through the people,** not by their own individual efforts alone. This is why leaders do not accept every task that a person might want to put on them.

Leaders carry the baton of the purposeful mission and compel others into action. They are *not* the pack mule.

Let's not forget that everything that was ever achieved that was larger than one person occurred because *"average"* people made it happen, not extraordinary people. However, behind the scenes, the only reason the "average" people made it happen is because leaders lead the way.

Humanity doesn't need more people who are extraordinary doers; it needs more leaders!

CHAPTER 30

Forward Progress Solves Hesitation

There is a truth so strange that it is hard to believe. Astute minds know that reality shows we can have mastery over our bodies and minds. If we decide we want ice cream, we compel our body up and towards the freezer to get it, and if we don't have it, we'll jump into a car, drive 20 minutes to a grocery store, purchase just the ice cream and return home with it, burning gallons of precious fuel for 1 gallon or less of ice cream.

We all *know* we can *just go do* anything we actually want to do. But for some reason, people go through life waiting for permission.

Hesitation is the inability to take action.

Hesitation is a natural reaction to uncertainty. (described in detail in the next chapter). Hesitation, as a psychological effect, impacts the ability to think clearly, to take initiative, and do the right thing.

Hesitation causes a person to put the least amount of energy into a task. When the task inevitably fails, they are reinforced in their hesitations.

We all know people that need to do certain actions to get their lives in order but simply won't. Some people need to have difficult conversations with their spouses; others need to begin highlighting the qualities in their spouse.

All people hesitate in one form or another.

But why?

Hesitation exists because leadership is not present

You may have been expecting a different reason as to why hesitation exists. You might stop for a moment and begin listing all the **reasons** why a person might feel hesitation. Such as…

- Because hard decisions require hard consideration.

- Because ideas need to be fully fleshed out.

- Because people don't know what to do.

Yet, these are all symptoms of hesitation.

Hesitation is a feeling, and like all feelings, it originates from the soul that is producing it, not from an extrinsic reality.

While all of the listed above *reasons* seem reasonable, these are ultimately excuses for not taking action.

Hesitation exists because forward progress has slowed or stopped, and there is minimal clarity on where one is going next. This is *why* hesitation exists.

Hesitation is present when a person believes there is no path forward and they're waiting for leadership to materialize. Accept people hesitate, but accept that something can be done about it.

Proof: Action commands dispel or create hesitation

Fundamental proof that "hesitation" is the lack of leadership is the power of action commands.

The fact that people *will* respond to commands that are intended to get them to cross the line and move forward is proof enough that hesitation is caused by a lack of leadership.

Why else would the simple act of saying **"GO"** get a person to move if it weren't for the **need** for a person to help them forward?

To make this clear for the reader, there are many people waiting on you.

Hesitation pools people up to the final line just before where they feel that they are "doing it." Instead of continuing forward, they stop and wait for the right "moment" to arrive. What they are waiting for is someone to help them cross over to the other side. To tell them… **"it's going to be OK, just do it."**

They know they want it; they know they want to progress, but they just don't know how to do it without the assistance in baby steps.

Let's consider for just a moment how absurd this phenomenon really is.

People dream up and fantasize about a future that they want (no matter how big or small) and then spend an inordinate amount of time dreaming about it, talking about it, and explaining away why they currently do not have it. Yet, just by the right person coming in and "giving them the permission", they begin to cross over the line from fantasy into reality.

People often continue to sit, idling by, **waiting** for someone to give them the nudge from behind to **"do it."**

Yet it's that simple.

It's the push from behind that gets us going. It is the baby steps, **the forward progress, that cures our hesitation.**

The reverse is true as well.

People come into our lives and tell us that we cannot do something, or we have to do X Y, or Z first. A million reasons and excuses are envisioned by the hesitant to stop us in our tracks from doing what we want to do.

It turns out that hesitation can be a contagious disease.

Even though we want the opposite, we still listen to them. But why would we ever listen to this?

Because in those moments we are hesitating!

Recognize Hesitation is Everywhere

If you stop for a moment and listen very carefully when people speak, you will see they are more than likely either frustrated or hesitating.

1. Is the person asking permission to do something?
2. Is the person trying to influence you to go do something *together*?
3. Is the person hemming and hawing?
4. Is the person explaining to you all the little details of why a problem exists and how it's impossible or so difficult to solve?
5. Is the person waiting around, waiting for someone else to do something, or waiting for someone to tell them what to do?

These people *are* hesitating!

For each of these situations, there are opposite examples where a person isn't hesitating. Here is the same list, turned around with people who are not hesitating.

1. The person is telling you what they are doing so that you have the ability to coordinate. (Note: They are not asking in such a way that they are seeking approval).

2. The person is stating where they are going and asking if you want to join them.

3. The person is direct with their statements or is trying to get more direct in their statements, or they are saying nothing at all. (Instead of listening and watching.)

4. The person provides as much detail as **other people desire and need** and instead spends the bulk majority of their speaking time on defining solutions.

5. The person is focused on getting something meaningful accomplished yet has the ear of those who need it.

These people are *NOT* hesitating.

What I am trying to get across to you is that you need to see in yourself and others when hesitation has taken hold. Instead of trying to "understand it", instead of trying to "rationalize it", just sweep it away and say, "it's going to be OK, just do it!"

Hesitation Is Opportunity

When people hesitate, that is the opportunity and an opening for leadership. But how do you seize these opportunities?

Start with Acceptance

Avoid getting lured into frustration. Many people, myself included, can get carried away by frustrations that people are simply not addressing their own hesitations. Start by accepting that hesitation is a natural process.

If you accept that hesitation happens, you will be able to see it and do something about it.

If people ask permission, get them to give *themselves* permission.

Sometimes it makes sense to give permission, but most of the time, consider getting how you can turn it around and get the person to give their own permission.

In almost every situation, if you are intentional enough, you can invert the energy of hesitant and permission-seeking people into personal power.

Let's take a look at a simple example with two people. We'll start with the beginning and then take a look at responses in four different ways.

Permission Seeking: "Can we go over there?"

Reply: "You want to go over there?"

Permission Seeking: "Yes, I do. I would like to see what they are doing."

At this point, let's take a look at four responses.

The Lack of Any Leadership

Reply: "I don't want to go over there."

Permission Seeking: "Oh, come on. Can't we just see what they are up to?"

Reply: "You can go; I want to go over there. Let's go over there!"

Permission Seeking: "Meh…"

Minimal Leadership

Reply: "What are you waiting for?"

Permission Seeking: "Well. I don't know. I'm just seeing if you want to go too?"

Reply: "Well, you can go."

Permission Seeking: "Well. I don't want to go if you don't want to go."

Taking Control – Just giving permission

Reply: Yes, we can go. Let's go.

Inversion and Empowering

Reply: "Do you think we can?"

Permission Seeking: "Of course. I don't see why not? All we have to do is go over there."

Reply: "What is stopping us?"

Permission Seeking: "Nothing."

Reply: "Are we going to go?"

Permission Seeking: "Yes. Let's go."

In the **"Lack of Any Leadership"** scenario, both people are trying, half-heartedly, to convince the other person to go in a direction without really listening to the person.

In the **"Minimum Leadership"** scenario, there is an attempt to determine what's the problem, but this is often unfruitful because it focuses on the problem rather than getting the person to *go do what they want.*

The **"Taking Control"** scenario is cut and dry. A decision is made, permission has been granted, and off they go. While this is good from a basic leadership perspective and often needed, there is a danger in this.

By tempting people with the fact that you can and will make decisions, all decisions start to fall on your shoulders. **This is deeply problematic in trying to achieve a purpose that is greater than yourself.**

Your bigger job is to influence people to take these responsibilities up, to include making decisions and leading people in a direction.

The **"Inversion and Empowering"** scenario attempts to get at the real problem. The problem is that the person is asking permission at all.

People ask permission of everyone around them, often trying to get approval rather than moving forward. You can do your part by asking if other people want to join you. In this last situation, the person inverts the discussion into one where the asker is the one who is stating that it is possible. As each question is asked, the "permission seeker" is more and more becoming the person who is the advocate of "yes it can be done, why are we waiting around?"

For some people, this is a painful experience to hand over the baton of decision making, but it a necessary step towards building leaders and scaling.

While there seems to be some "judo" convincing in the discussion, try to avoid thinking of it as maneuvering around the person, and instead consider the question as a genuine attempt to understand "why is this person asking permission?"

Instead of trying to dig into the hesitations, the question of **"do you think we can"** get the other person to be a driver instead of a recipient.

Seek out Hesitancy Through Genuine Questions

Whether or not you are aware of it, people are hesitant. Depending on how you have organized your life, people may even be hesitant to bring up issues with you. Fixing this comes from asking questions and seeking them out.

These hesitant areas are ripe for taking action on to earn influence.

Move Beyond Permission

Creating and cultivating an environment where permission is minimal with high initiative is the gold standard of effectiveness. But it takes consistency to occur.

Building *this* kind of culture requires, from the top down, reminding ourselves of the environment that we are building. As you convince yourself of this, others will become convinced. As others become convinced, they will convince others.

In order to have a culture that takes action, you have to have an environment that cultivates and rewards the behavior of moving beyond permission.

> "It is Better to Ask for
> Forgiveness than Permission."

Leaders who are looking to empower action regularly make this statement. Say it boldly and with intent. It is empowering and creates a culture of responsibility, effectiveness, and initiative.

In order to take it beyond a saying, leaders need to resist the urge to punish for mistakes. Mistakes can and will be costly, but **mistakes are the necessary cost for building strength, capability, and experience.**

It is our natural instincts to feel frustrated by setbacks, which is why we want to "seek permission". But we have to channelize this into learning from our mistakes and taking another initiative.

Lastly, Remind Others to Go with Their Gut Instincts When It Feels Compelling

While going with your gut instincts all the time is not the best decision, when your gut instincts are compelling, you need to listen. When your gut instincts call on you so strongly that you feel that you "must do something" other than "the plan", you need to listen to it **because there are real rewards for doing so and punishments for ignoring it.**

Effective leaders reinforce others to trust their instincts and do what they know they ought to do. If a person feels compelled, there is a deep need to fulfill this desire. *These are the situations in which you truly learn what you know.*

Removing hesitations is on the path to
personal leadership.

CHAPTER 31

Help People Clear Uncertainty

Last but not least, it is one of the most important summations of what a leader ought to know about people. Uncertainty is one of the most detrimental conditions, and yet it is consistently overlooked and under-examined by leaders.

Uncertainty is a chronic fear.

Uncertainty is the physiological feeling of not being able to anticipate what is happening or could happen. This type of concern can encircle a person's thinking and cause them to expend all of their energies in its service.

While similar to hesitation, uncertainty is felt across people and tends to saturate an environment. Uncertainty is often passed among people like a virulent disease until dispelled by someone who "brings" certainty. The condition of uncertainty can be sensed, felt, and observed by watching the topics, actions, and mannerisms of those under its spell. Like other emotions, uncertainty cannot be easily "explained" or rationalized away, but rather the root causes must be addressed.

Uncertainty causes people to constantly shift

The primary effect of uncertainty is fidgeting. While at first, this may seem like a laughing matter to discuss, the fidgeting from uncertainty will cause people to start taking actions that have detrimental effects on themselves, those they care about, and the organizations that they are supporting.

These types of fidgeting include:

- A complete drop in productivity, instead of focusing entirely on "what may happen next".
- Preemptively leaving a job they feel they will soon lose.
- Conducting offensive actions against other people out of fear, such as taking legal or violent actions against them.
- Causing drama with people around them, such as adopting outlandish beliefs about each person.
- Seeking outside counsel instead of counsel from those within their circle of influence.

This "fidgeting" completely hollows out the productiveness of organizations and teams.

Uncertainty is created because of leadership voids.

Uncertainty is so tightly bound to leadership that it bears stating plainly that uncertainty only exists in the absence of leadership. That is when people are no longer being influenced to work towards honorable, purposeful ends, whether internally or externally, inevitably people cave in.

> Dispelling uncertainty by providing clarity,
> and keeping a healthy vision alive, is the most
> important service that a leader can provide.

People ultimately begin to fear that which they cannot see. If people cannot get an understanding of what is in front of them, they begin to fill in the blanks themselves. Most of the time it is not enough to speak to a person to dispel uncertainty. However, showing them information that is curated on paper and the example you personally live are quite compelling methods.

In 2020 the Belief of Collapse is Everywhere

This void is why in the year 2020, the feeling of uncertainty is everywhere. There is a constant belief, *everywhere*, that people are going to lose their jobs, that the economy is going to collapse, that World War 3 is going to happen any minute, an apocalypse is around the corner, a super virus-bacteria will kill everyone, that "big government" is spying on them in that moment, the planet is collapsing, and in the end, everyone is doomed.

There is clearly a leadership crisis. Where are we going? Nowhere? I guess that means we're all dead!

This environment of uncertainty is allowing an unprecedented level of predation to occur.

Perhaps never in human history has safety and security been a bigger drain of resources than today. There is no shortage of examples of resource depletion from uncertainty, such as the global bureaucratic military-industrial complex and the growing gargantuan cybersecurity industry to even at the personal level with the sales of firearms and home intrusion systems.

Even though statistics prove that human life has never been better, uncertainty is building and growing regardless.

When leaders become uncertain, that is when the people really become concerned.

Like other human conditions, "monkey see monkey do" truly takes over with uncertainty. Uncertain leaders are the worst offenders of propagating, creating, and sowing the seeds of uncertainty.

Be careful following people who radiate uncertainty.

Regardless of the problems that exist, there is always a way to survive. There is always something that can and should be done about it. There is always the need to face it rather than run away from it. This is why you must begin dispelling uncertainty by being a force for the future.

Five Ways to Detect Uncertainty

If you enter into a new situation, here are five ways to determine the levels of uncertainty in the environment.

1. Do people change directions often?
2. Are the leaders charging a path to achieving something?
3. Do people incessantly go on and on and on about the problems there and point to detail after detail?
4. Do regular loyal folks talk about leaving and finding somewhere better?
5. Is there an overall lack of belief in a positive future?

Occupations are saturated in these types of environments. The best thing you can bring to this table is building relationships with people and start to chart a course for success. **It works.**

If you grow in leadership, you can dispel uncertainty

Uncertainty is cleared by leaders. Leaders chart paths that are compelling and clearly stated. You can do it, and you should start now.

If the people are uncertain around you, **whether you think of yourself as a leader currently or not,** this ought to be a sign that you need to rise from where you are and bring certainty by pointing in the direction of where everyone ought to be going, take a step in that direction, and encourage others to follow.

Move Forward, Earn Forward Progress

People can intuitively feel if they are moving forward. Moving forward helps creates happiness and fulfillment in people's lives. It is the momentum that they feel, and when it is momentum gained from forward progress, they are more willing to take steps to earn on that momentum.

> If you don't know how to move forward, you
> need to start at the basics. Make your bed.
> Clean your house. Get others to join in just
> cleaning up and organizing the world at your
> fingertips. Don't just tell others to do it, be
> the one who is doing it and invite others in.

You have to understand your psychology requires reducing uncertainty

If you allow uncertainty to dangle and invade your mind, it will cause you harm. If you are leading people, this will be amplified out onto the people. You can only hide for so long that you are uncertain, as your actions and behaviors will give off the sign of a person who is uncertain.

One of the best ways to clear uncertainty is to prepare what you are going to say to others. It takes work but being able to speak succinctly on "what is happening" and "what needs to be done" can embolden people to adopt an action behavior.

This is a sight to be seen if you haven't seen it before.

People who are lacking certainty create a lot of discussion and back and forth. **The back and forth requires an uncertain ground for people to banter over.**

People respond completely differently when they interact with a person who has deep conviction, and part of their conviction is that "we all need to work on this" and "we need you to do this for us."

Even if you do not have a grand vision that you are driving the whole world into success over, if you can provide people these experiences, they will **know** they're making a difference.

Clearing uncertainty is a Leader's #2 Job

A leader's job is ultimately to find the right people and put them together; the second job is to clear uncertainty. This is why I have labored over the topic of uncertainty and left it as the final topic regarding people.

When people sign up to be a follower, here are a few questions they ask, not with words but from their behavior:

1. Where are we all going?
2. What will it look like when we get there?
3. What is the topography we will be crossing?
4. Which dangers do we need to be on the lookout for?
5. How should we conduct ourselves, internally and externally?

People need a vision on these questions. especially if there are changes that are needed in where they are now.

Ultimately, people want to know that where they are going will be better, and they know they need to be prepared before making the change.

> Until people have firm ideas in their mind about what is next in their lives, they will be eaten away by uncertainty. "What if, what if what if, maybe?" Leaders everywhere need to resolve uncertainty issues because it saps away the strength of the team while they wait to realize this is their job.

Notes

In Closing

The mantle of real leadership can be a heavy burden to bear, yet you will be rewarded in small continual ways and with occasional grand moments; if there was ever a time for the awakening of your leadership, it's now.

This text ought to have provided you enough different and new aspects that you might understand how at least a few of these aspects are missing throughout human existence as you know it.

Leadership can change the positive trajectory of every relationship you have. Powerful, compelling, and meaningful relationships with others are within your grasp. Those whom you encounter can and should always be directed into the service of the ends that you desire.

While every person can be influenced, not every person should accompany you on your long journey.

To accompany you on the long road, you need to commit to others for them to commit to your path. Remember that your influence and leadership have different qualities with different people. Whether it's your parents, spouse, friends, coworkers, internet trolls, or random strangers, all of them require different influencing. Those who care about you personally *will* join your journey **because it's what you give them**. Others will join because it is *that* particular journey.

There are leadership vacuums in every organization, especially those that are the loudest about leadership. They have "servant leadership" written on their documents, yet they never ask their employees, "is there anything I can help with? What are the problems?"

Our workplaces are missing purpose, honor, and courage. There is no better way to see the effects of purpose-less existence than to step back and look around. How people carry themselves, the entitlements that people demand, the lack of cohesion with others, and rampant uncertainty and fear there is little doubt people need a bit of lifting up in overt and subtle ways.

These people are not in teams that are working together with an upward trajectory. These people are not in your presence.

Where there is chaos, there is your opportunity

Instead of allowing momentum to take place, causing people to feel disconnected, aimless, and open to predation of the vices of the world, you can bring them light and point to a better direction.

Make no mistake; it is possible for you to soak up the lost spirits of the world and put them in order for your vision. **This is what a lost soul is looking for; a purpose to be guided towards. They want to feel like they are part of** *something* **rather than a** *repetitive nothing.*

If you've made it this far, you have it in you to guide them.

You may even still have your doubts

Will people really respond to these "tricks?" Are people really telling me their underlying emotions every time they speak? Is everyone really that different but still the same?

If it is true that we cannot influence the belief in others until we are able to influence the belief in ourselves, then it calls upon us to personally experience **what is true first.**

Take this book and put it to the test intentionally.

If the small tips, recommendations, and observations work out, you can then understand the larger truth behind this book.

> It is true, the world is your oyster, and everyone is
> a chess piece within it.

Summary

In order to be able to remember the key lessons of the book, here is a summary list of all of the core concepts.

Know the Foundations of Leadership

Leadership is the practice of earning influence for the purpose of compelling others to do actions. It is the only way for you to accomplishing something larger.

Influence, a natural phenomenon, arises from a belief that a person will be able to reach something they desire *if* they do the actions that lead in a particular direction.

Force is the act of coercing someone to do an action. It works by creating or reinforcing an immediate sense of fear.

Fear is the feeling felt by a person when they believe "if I don't do this, then bad things will happen to me."

Using force, while effective at compelling small and immediate actions, is exceptionally costly, cannot be sustained, and prevents receiving the efforts of a full person engaged in a common struggle.

We all are able to be influenced because we are looking for others to validate what we believe and show us a way to obtain that which we want most.

Manipulation never has the ability to obtain something greater than oneself.

Planning can make actions more effective, but it is not a replacement for action.

Words are actions; however, because they are easy to use, words are commonly used ineffectually.

Leadership is the practice of conducting continual and strategic actions that earn influence with others, which is then used to compel persons into wisely chosen actions that have an honorable purposeful end.

In order to become a leader, you must adopt an attitude of growth, be of good character, have genuine concern for the well-being of others, and continually seek progress towards a purposeful end.

To effectively lead, you need to understand the complexities of how people operate, become aware of these peculiarities in yourself, and assist in searching for and maximizing the expression of each person's innate qualities.

Influence Yourself

Your character is your most influential and fundamental quality.

Your character influences you first; then, your actions influence others.

Improving your character changes your trajectory.

The actions we choose come from the values that we actually possess. Choosing different values yields different actions, which yields different effects on our influence.

You should learn and practice the Marine Corps Leadership Traits because by performing actions that come from holding these as values, you will miraculously earn influence.

1. Justice	8. Enthusiasm
2. Judgment	9. Bearing
3. Dependability	10. Unselfishness
4. Initiative	11. Courage
5. Decisiveness	12. Knowledge
6. Tact	13. Loyalty
7. Integrity	14. Endurance

You should learn and adopt the Marine Corps Leadership principles, like the traits; using them will ensure that everyone, yourself included, believes that you are a leader and will set you up to earn and spend influence for the right reasons.

1. Know Yourself and Seek Self Improvement
2. Be Technically and Tactically Proficient
3. Know Your People and Look Out For Their Welfare
4. Keep Your Personnel Informed
5. Set the Example
6. Ensure That the Task Is Understood, Supervised, and Accomplished
7. Train Your Subordinates as a Team
8. Make Sound and Timely Decisions
9. Employ Your Command within its Capabilities
10. Seek Responsibilities and Take Responsibility

You can change your values over time by carrying them with you in your pocket. Look at them daily, tell others that you possess those values, and watch magically how you eventually will.

If you do actions that you receive no benefit from, you'll free yourself from negative habits.

Begin reflecting on your actions from a fair perspective. Consider situations you have performed poorly in, and then think about how one that possesses certain values might act. Adopt those habits.

Challenge yourself in order to gain personal respect.

Seek out purpose and meaning to give an emotional backing to why your efforts matter.

Learning how to feel invulnerable will protect you from the need to be defensive, giving you space to focus on others.

Earn Influence with Others

People either follow you, or they don't. Influence is earned and cannot be given.

Influence works similar to money. As you earn influence with a person, you can ask for larger actions from them. If you overspend, then it causes relationship issues.

Be careful of accepting gifts from others because you are spending influence without intending to.

Influence is earned from actions recognized by the recipient.

Your actions should show you care for the other person.

Do continuous small actions because you will not always know which actions will have the biggest impact.

Put together strategies to earn great influence.

Having an interest in another person and asking questions related to what they want to talk about is the easiest way to earn influence.

Questions are an effective way to earn influence continually if they are directed at raising the value of other people.

To ask powerful questions, consider asking:

1. Direct questions.

2. Ones that incite emotional replies

3. Difficult questions that you feel hesitation asking

4. Open-ended questions

Listening is one of the most important skills you can learn in leadership.

Listening consists of Passive and Active forms. Consider using passive listening if you feel that you do not want to take the chance of modifying what the person is saying by your presence. Use active listening when you want to dig in and really understand what a person is wanting to communicate.

Technical content is the literal words that a person communicates.

Intent is the exact message that a person is actually trying to convey.

Emotional content is what the person feels, which is driving the desire to communicate.

To gain the skill in empathy while earning influence, say out loud the emotion that the other person is experiencing.

Delegation can be an effective form of earning influence.

Some general strategies for earning influence continually and strategically are:

1. Becoming an educator

2. Becoming a manager

3. Becoming a top performer

4. Becoming an advocate

5. Becoming a networker

6. Becoming a good person

Spending Influence

Any time we ask others to adopt an idea, perform an action, or ask others to carry a burden, we expend our influence to do so.

This includes the times that we are not aware that we are doing so.

When you run out of influence, you meet resistance.

Wise Action – Good Experience and Good Judgment

Wise actions are ones that bring the straightest path to what you are trying to achieve.

Wisdom can answer the what, where, when, who, and how questions.

Listen first and speak last.

Since time is always moving forward, you must act as wisely as you can against the clock of life.

Pick your victory's "Musts", "Shoulds", and "Nice to Haves" carefully. They determine the amount of effort necessary and only come from clear thinking.

Avoid solving problems that do not have to do with what success requires.

Tasks are specific actions that we can do, while outcomes are the desired end results of our actions. Know the difference.

Wisdomless decisions come from a lack of holistic thinking.

To think wiser, begin thinking strategically, consider separating yourself from others, and learn how to manage money.

Purposeful Action – A reason for existence

Purpose is the distillation of "who you are" and "what you value."

Purpose can only be found through discovery.

Once you have discovered purpose, begin to communicate it to others continually.

Help others to own the purpose and empower them to drive it for you.

Attempting to lead people without telling them why is manipulation. It is costly to your influence and unwise.

People flounder if they do not know why they are doing what they are doing. Yes, you have to tell them.

Without purpose, people will blame you for anything and everything.

In order to discover purpose, consider spending time in nature, around children, or around death.

Honorable Action – Of High Respect

Honorable actions are actions that express a person's highest values.

Leaders exist to push, pull, cajole, or otherwise get people to do the actions that they know they ought to perform.

Honorable actions aren't "why", but "should" and "must" actions.

Choosing an honorable path, insulates your followers from toxic outside cultures; instead, it builds momentum and eventually legacy.

Take care, unless it is your will, in accidentally choosing honor to be your purpose, as unbridled idealism can take root in your followers if you have it as well.

Practical Tips on Spending Influence

Practice tasking people.

Learn to give commands without being asked and without asking.

Learn to ask for action. "Will you do this?" or "can you do this?"

By moving faster in life, people will get a sense of "urgency" in the environment.

Keep tabs on how much you ask of others.

Improve your communication through courses and practice.

Hire another person to conduct small labor for you, just so you have experience bringing wise and honorable purpose to another.

Become an Effective Leader

People are very different. – Engage with others based on what they care about.

People are the same. – Help people change by positively impacting their lives.

People Believe and Have Faith – If you expand people's beliefs, it will expand their actions.

People are Their Habits. – If you or people you know need a higher trajectory, change their habits.

Life Adapts to its Environment – You have to shape the environment so that it is conducive to funneling people in a direction.

Hierarchies have powerful amplifying influence effects – Consider encouraging and helping other people to lead.

People are #1 Infatuated with Themselves – Earn the starter influence you need by praising others and lending an ear to what other people want to talk about; however, get them to get out of their world to help others for a lasting effect.

People Want to Know and Use Powerful People– Be selective in doing the tasks others ask of you, especially once you have established yourself as a person who can get things done. Instead, try to empower the other person to get their own work done. (How else could you get so much accomplished?)

People Hesitate – Whenever you sense hesitation from anyone, or there is negativity that is grinding action to a halt, it is an opportunity for you to figure out a way to get people to take baby steps in the direction they need to go in.

People Drown in Uncertainty – Uncertainty is created in a leadership void, not the "things" that are blamed for creating uncertainty. Gain self-awareness to ensure you are the one eliminating uncertainty by shepherding people instead of causing it or propagating it. If you are confident about moving forward, other people will become that as well.

Notes

www.ingramcontent.com/pod-product-compliance
Lightning Source LLC
Chambersburg PA
CBHW031244090426
42742CB00007B/304

* 9 7 8 1 7 3 6 6 8 2 6 0 9 *